LAS VEGAS

SILBERSTANG'S GUIDE
TO POKER

SILBERSTANG'S

GUIDE TO POKER

Edwin Silberstang

A PERIGEE BOOK

Perigee Books
are published by
The Putnam Publishing Group
200 Madison Avenue
New York, NY 10016

Library of Congress Cataloging-in-Publication Data

Silberstang, Edwin, date.
  Silberstang's Guide to poker.

  1. Poker I. Title. II. Title: Guide to poker.
GV1251.S39   1985   795.41'2   85-12400
ISBN 0-399-51176-8

Printed in the United States of America
1   2   3   4   5   6   7   8   9   10

For Henry Toledano

CONTENTS

INTRODUCTION

Poker is one of the most interesting and exciting games that one can play. It's a game of skill that blends elements of luck and psychology. It's a great money game, and there are a number of men and women who play this game professionally. It is also enjoyable as an occasional game, and whether played for blood or for enjoyment, it has something for everyone.

In this book, we'll cover the basics of the most popular poker games and variations, showing how these games are played. But that's not all we'll do. We'll go deeper and further, showing the correct methods of play and the strategies that will make one a winner at the game.

The study and practice of correct poker strategies will be rewarding, not only in money but also in the knowledge that one is playing well and beating others at a game of skill.

Poker is played against other players, never against the house, not even when you are playing in a casino. The casino runs the game, but the players compete against one another, so if you become skilled at the game, there's no way a casino will be able to bar you from play, as it may do when you play against it directly in its table games, such as blackjack.

Some players like to concentrate on one particular variation of poker; others can play most games of poker well. They're all in here for you to study and learn; draw and stud, five- and seven-card, high and low and high-low. There's also a chapter on Texas Hold 'Em, one of the fastest-growing popular forms of poker around, played in many of the Nevada casinos.

Learn the games. If you already know the fundamentals, this book is still for you, because the strategies considered have been used by top winners at this game. By the time you're finished, you'll be a winner at whatever form of poker you desire to play.

SILBERSTANG'S GUIDE
TO POKER

I

THE BASIC RULES OF POKER

THE DECK OF CARDS

Poker is played with the fifty-two-card pack, the same pack used for such games as bridge. There are four suits: spades (S), hearts (H), diamonds (D), and clubs (C). The suits have no effect on the value of a hand; the important value is in the ranking of the cards within the suits.

Each suit contains thirteen cards. Ranked in order of strength, from strongest to weakest, they are ace, king, queen, jack, 10, 9, 8, 7, 6, 5, 4, 3, 2.

The king (K), queen (Q), and jack (J) are known as "face" cards, or as "paint." They rank just below the ace, and will have the appropriate symbol ("K," "Q," or "J") printed in two of the corners. All the other cards can be distinguished by the number in two of the corners, which numbers refer to the spots on the card. A 5 of diamonds will have the number 5 printed in red in two corners, and will also have five diamonds or spots on the card itself. The 10 of spades will have 10 printed on the corners and have ten spades drawn on the card itself. One need not count the spots; the number on the corners is sufficient. Spades and clubs have traditionally been the black suits; hearts and diamonds the red suits.

The ace is the most powerful card in poker, and is usually embellished by the designer of the card in some unique manner, especially the ace of spades. Otherwise there will be an "A" in two corners of the card, plus a single suit symbol on the card, in the center. There's no mistaking an ace, for the symbol "A" is used instead of a number.

The ace sets the limits of the hands in poker. For example, if a player holds a straight (that is, five cards of any suits that are in consecutive order, such as ace, 2, 3, 4, and 5), the ace is the lowest card that can be used for a straight. On the other hand, the highest card in a straight is also the ace and the highest possible straight in poker is the 10, jack, queen, king, and ace. This is known as an "ace-high" straight.

When an ace is used for a flush (that is, five cards in the player's hand all of the same suit), the ace automatically is the highest-ranking card. Thus a flush consisting of ace, queen, 7, 5, 3 would be an "ace-high" flush.

In certain instances, the ace is the lowest-ranking card. We saw one instance in which an ace, 2, 3, 4, 5 straight makes the ace the lowest-ranking card. That straight would be known as a "5-high" straight, the lowest-ranking straight in "high" poker. A "6-high" or any other straight will beat this "5-high" straight.

However, there are "low" forms of poker, in which the object is to get the lowest possible hand. In "low" poker, the best possible hand is a "5-high" straight, with the ace counting as the lowest card, equal to a 1. In "low" poker, the ace again is the most powerful card, not because of its high, but because of its low value.

To recapitulate: The ace is the highest-ranking card in the deck, except when making a low straight or in "low" forms of poker. The rank order of the other cards is (from high to low) king (K), queen (Q), jack (J), 10, 9, 8, 7, 6, 5, 4, 3, 2. The suits have no effect on a hand's value, and the two jokers that come with every new deck of cards are not used, but are discarded from the pack.

THE HAND

In poker, when we refer to "a hand" we're referring to the cards the player is holding. There are games in which a player will be dealt six or seven cards, and others in which he'll be dealt two cards and will form his hand with exposed "community" cards that are in the center of the table. In either case, he will use only five cards to form his hand. If dealt six or seven cards, he'll make his hand from the best five cards he holds. If playing in a game where he is dealt only two cards, as in Texas Hold 'Em, he'll combine his two cards with three of the community cards "on the board" to make his hand.

The hand will thus be only five cards, and there is a good reason for this. In practically all forms of poker, and certainly in all forms of poker we'll be discussing in this book, the relative rank of the hands depends on a five-card holding, or hand. The sixth or seventh card, even though dealt or seen, is superfluous to the hand.

For example, suppose, in a seven-card game, the player is dealt king, king, 9, 9, 6, 6 and ace. His best five-card holding would be the two kings and the two 9s with the ace. The kings are his highest-ranking pair; the 9s the second-highest pair, and the ace is the highest-ranking odd card. If another player held two kings, two 9s and a queen, for example, the player with the odd ace would beat that other hand. All other cards in the first player's hand are superfluous; thus he wouldn't count the 6s in showing his best possible hand.

Before we show the relative rankings of the hands in poker, let's first discuss the object of the game.

OBJECT OF THE GAME

Poker is basically a money game. If you do not play for stakes the game can be boring, because when nothing is at stake, the skill and the psychological aspects of poker go for naught, and the game loses its unique flavor.

The object of the game is to win the money in the pot on any round of play. The pot is the total of money derived from antes and bets on any round of play. (Antes and bets will be described in full later on.) During the play, money will be placed by the competing players in the center of the table and will accumulate through the rounds of play till the end of play, and its total will be known as the pot.

There are several ways a player can win the pot. First, if all the other players drop out of the round of play and leave him alone, then he will have the pot to himself, and can withdraw all the money from it and put it on his personal stacks.

This may occur as follows: Suppose on the second round of play, after some money has already been bet and anted, the player shows a pair of aces, very strong cards. If this is a game of high poker, the holder of the aces makes the first bet. He puts out his chips and no one calls (matches) the bet. All the other players "fold," (turn over their cards and drop out), so that the holder of the two aces is the only player left. He claims and collects the pot.

Sometimes a player will "bluff" the other players out of the game by making a big bet even though he doesn't have the best cards. Giving the appearance that you have the best hand by making a large bet is known as bluffing. If all the other players fold, the bluffer can then claim the pot without showing his cards.

The usual way one wins a pot is by having the best hand at the "showdown," after all the cards have been dealt and all bets made. At this point, the last player to be called first shows his cards, and if they're best, the others in the game can concede without showing theirs. If another player has a better (higher-ranking) hand, he can show his cards and claim the pot. A showdown always occurs when at least two players remain to the end.

To summarize: A player wins the pot when he forces out all the other players by betting or bluffing, or when, at the showdown, he has the best or highest-ranking of the hands of those remaining in the game.

If, at the showdown, two players remain with identical hands, it's a standoff, with the remaining players splitting the pot between them if they both have the highest hands. For example, if three players remained at the showdown, two holding a 10-high straight and the third two pairs, the holders of the 10-high straights would split the pot between them. The holder of the two pair, having a lower-ranking hand, would get nothing.

RANKING OF THE HANDS—HIGH POKER

The ranking of the hands in poker follows the laws of probability. The most difficult hand to get, by the laws of probability, is a royal flush, which consists of the ace, king, queen, jack and 10 of any one suit. (A royal flush in spades won't have precedence over one in diamonds, for example, because suits have no intrinsic value in poker.)

The ranking is based on the assumption that no wild card is used in the deck. A wild card is one designated to represent whatever card the player wishes it to represent. Sometimes a joker is used, or more often, some of the cards already in the pack, such as the 2s, are considered wild.

When a wild card is used in the pack, the highest-ranking hand is no longer a royal flush, but five of a kind. For example, if a player held the four 9s and held a wild card with them, he could designate that wild card as a 9, and the hand could be read as five 9s, or five of a kind. This hand would have precedence over all other hands, except, of course, another five-of-a-kind hand of higher rank, such as five 10s.

But leaving wild cards aside, let's now examine the ranking of hands in high poker, from the highest on down.

Royal Flush

This is the best hand to get in poker, and is made up of the ace, king, queen, jack, and 10 of one suit only.

Example: Ace (C), king (C), queen (C), jack (C), and 10 (C). If two players at the showdown both had royal flushes, the pot would be split between them.

Straight Flush

It's very rare to see a royal flush, but from time to time straight flushes are dealt in games. The straight flush combines a flush and a straight in one hand. For example, the following is a straight flush: jack(S), 10(S), 9(S), 8(S), 7(S).

All hands are subject to the ranks of the cards, and if two players held straight flushes, one headed by a queen and the other by a jack, the queen-high straight flush would win. The lowest possible straight flush is the 5-high, consisting of the 5, 4, 3, 2, and ace of the same suit. In this case, the ace is counted as a 1, or the lowest card.

If two players have straight flushes of equal rank, for example, both 8-high, the pot is split between them.

Four of a Kind

When a player holds four cards of the same rank, such as four aces or four 2s, he has a four-of-a-kind hand, the third-best in high poker.

Any four-of-a-kind hand would consist of cards of four different suits, such as 3(S), 3(H), 3(D), and 3(C).

The fifth card will not be important, for there is no way that two players can have the same four-of-a-kind hand. The hand of the higher-ranked cards, if two players have four-of-a-kind hands, will win the pot. For example, four kings will best four queens.

Full House

A full house, or full boat, as it is sometimes called, consists of three of a kind and a pair in the same hand. For example, if a player held three 4s and two aces, that would be a full house. Other examples might be three queens and two kings, or JJJ55, or 6661010.

In determining the winner of any pot when two or more players have full houses, the rank of the three of a kind in each hand alone is considered. For example, if one player held QQQ66 and the other JJJAA, the three-queen hand would win the pot.

There are no ties between full houses. To make certain that the player announces his hand correctly, the usual manner of calling a full house is to state the three of a kind in the hand and say "full" afterward. For example, if a player held 44499, he would establish its value by saying "4s full."

However, even if he misstates his hand, as sometimes happens, the cards will "speak for themselves," and when laid down at the showdown, the highest-ranking full house will win the pot even if incorrectly stated.

Flush

A five-card holding in one suit only, though not in any consecutive order, is a flush. For example, if a player has jack(S), 9(S), 8(S), 6(S), 3(S), he holds a jack-high flush. When announcing the value of a flush, or showing it, the best practice is to set the cards in order of rank, so that its value is immediately apparent to the other players.

When two or more players hold flushes, the highest-ranking flush wins the pot. The highest flush is an ace-high

19

one. Thus, an ace-high flush will beat all other flushes. A queen-high flush will beat all but king- or ace-high flushes.

When two players hold the same-ranking high card in their respective flushes, such as king-high, the next-ranking card in the flush is looked at to determine the winner. For example, if one player holds king, jack, 10, 5, and 3 of clubs and the other holds king, 10, 9, 8, and 7 of hearts, the club flush will win, for it is king-jack, while the heart flush is only king-10.

Sometimes not only are the highest-ranking cards identical, but the second and third cards in rank are also identical. In that case, the fourth-ranking card will have to be looked at, and if that is identical, then the fifth-ranking card will be examined to determine the winner. For example, a queen, 10, 9, 7, 4 flush will beat a queen, 10, 9, 7, 3 flush.

If two players left at the showdown hold completely identical flushes, the pot will be split.

Straight

A straight may be defined as any five consecutive cards of random suits. For example, an ace(C), king(D), queen(D), jack(H), 10(S) is an ace-high straight. However, when the hand is composed of 5, 4, 3, 2, and ace, it is a 5-high straight, and the ace is counted as the lowest card. The ace is lowest in high poker only in this instance, when counting it toward a low straight headed by the 5.

As mentioned previously, the ace can only be the highest or lowest card of a straight. A hand consisting of jack, queen, king, ace, and 2 is not a straight. If of different suits, the hand is a "no-pair" hand, of little value.

When two players hold straights at the showdown, the highest-ranking straight wins the pot. An ace-high straight is the highest, and will beat any other straight. If another player also holds an ace-high straight the pot will be split between the two straight-holders, as it will with any equally high straights.

Three of a Kind

When a player holds three cards of equal rank, along with two other odd cards, he has three of a kind. For example, the following hands are three-of-a-kind hands: 888KA, 444J3, JJJ95. In all these instances, there are two odd cards as well as three of a kind. This type of hand is also called triplets, or "trips."

There can be no ties when two or more players hold "trips." The holder of the highest-ranked three-of-a-kind hand wins the pot.

Two Pair

With this holding, the player has two separate pairs of cards of equal rank, along with one odd card. For example, the following hands are considered two-pair holdings: JJ88A, AAKK4, QQ332, 77665. The hands are placed so that the higher-ranked pair comes first. Thus, the four hands illustrated would be called, at the showdown, "jacks up," "aces up," "queens up," and "7s up." The fifth card will be odd in all instances.

If two or more players hold two-pair hands at the showdown, the winner of the pot will be the holder of the highest-ranking first pair. Thus kings up will beat queens up. Aces up is always the highest-ranking two-pair hand.

When the highest-ranking pairs are equal—for instance if two players hold queens up—the next pair is taken into consideration to see who wins the pot. Suppose one player has QQ994, and the other holds QQ88A. As the 9s are of higher rank than the 8s, the holder of the QQ994 hand would win the pot.

If both the first- and second-ranking pairs are identical,

the odd card is taken into consideration to determine who wins the pot. For example, if one player holds KK227 and the other KK226, the first hand wins, because the 7 is higher in rank than the 6. If all five cards are identical, the pot is split.

One Pair

This hand consists of two cards of equal rank along with three odd cards. For example, KK983, QQJ54, 77AKQ, and 33Q94 are all single- or one-pair hands.

When two or more players hold one pair at the showdown, the highest-ranking pair wins the pot. Aces are the highest ranking at all times. Should two players hold identical high pairs, the highest of the odd cards is taken into consideration to see which player wins the pot. For instance, AAQ92 beats AAJ98.

However, if the first odd cards (that is, the highest odd card in both hands) are identical, the next-highest odd card is taken into consideration, and if that is also the same rank, the third odd card is examined to determine the winner. KK643 beats KK642, because the final odd card in the first hand, the 3, is higher than the 2 in the second hand.

If all five cards are identical in rank, the pot is split.

No Pairs

This holding of five odd cards is the lowest in high poker. With this hand, the player has no two cards of equal rank, and his holding consists of two or more suits. If the five cards were odd, but all of one suit, it would be a flush. Also, the five odd cards can't be in consecutive order, for then the hand would be a straight.

The following are no-pair hands. (We'll show the suits to determine that the hands aren't flushes. A player should also do this when examining his holdings, for sometimes one can overlook a flush when looking at five odd cards.) A(D), 10(C), 8(S), 7(S), 6(S) and Q(D), J(D), 9(C), 4(H), 2(D) are both no-pair hands consisting of five odd cards. When two or more players hold no-pairs at the showdown, the player with the highest-ranking card in his hand wins the pot. If one player holds an ace, and none of his opponents hold one, that player will win the pot.

If two or more players hold identical high-ranking cards, the second-ranking card is taken into consideration to determine the winner of the pot. If these cards are identical, the third card is examined, and so forth, till a winner is determined. If all five cards are identical in rank, the pot is split.

A final note: Hands of equal strength should be examined for the highest-ranking card only when those hands are the highest-ranking hands at the showdown. If one player holds a straight and two other players hold one-pair hands, the straight will win, and there's no reason to examine the relative value or ranking of the one-pair hands. If two players held straights and the third held a one-pair hand the straights *would* be examined for relative ranking, with the winner being the player holding the higher-ranking straight.

II

HOW POKER IS PLAYED

THE DEAL

In all games of poker, there must be a dealer who gives out the cards, or "deals" them to the participants. In home games and in the California poker parlors, the dealer is one of the players. In the Nevada casinos, the dealer is an employee of the casino.

When one of the participants deals the cards, he deals cards to himself as well as to the other players. When an employee of a casino deals cards, the employee doesn't receive cards and stays out of the game.

Except in the casino game, where an employee is present dealing hands, the players take turns with the deal. It moves clockwise around the table, with each player getting a turn at dealing. With the deal come privileges and obligations. In certain games, such as draw poker, the dealer acts and bets last, and this is an advantage. In most other poker games, especially those in which some of the player's cards are exposed, there is no advantage, just the chore of dealing correctly.

DEALER'S OBLIGATIONS

The dealer's first obligation is to shuffle the cards so that they are randomly placed in the deck. After the cards are thoroughly shuffled, they're given to the player on the dealer's right to be cut. If that player refuses to cut the cards, another player can cut them before they're dealt.

Once the cards are restacked after the cut, the dealer begins his deal, giving out one card at a time, the first one going to the player on his left, and one to each other player in the game, and finally one to himself. After the requisite cards are dealt before the first betting round, the dealer retains the remaining pack or stock of cards and keeps these cards under his surveillance and control at all times.

In draw poker, five cards will be dealt, one at a time, to each player before the betting begins. In stud poker, two or three cards will be dealt before the first round of betting begins, some face up and some face down. If the game is stud, or open poker, the dealer calls the game, stating which player must bet first. Then he must make certain that the betting is in sequence. Each dealer runs the game during the time he is dealer.

In any game in which an ante is used, that is, money is put into the center of the table before the deal, to "sweeten" the pot, the dealer must make sure that all the players have anted the correct amount.

When players draw additional cards, as in draw poker, or drop out of the game in draw or stud poker, the dealer must gather the discards and place them to one side, out of play. Then he must advise which player bets first and keep track of the correct sequence of bets.

ANTES

We briefly mentioned antes and how they "sweeten" the pot. They aren't bets, and all players, in certain forms of home games, such as draw poker, and in casino games, must ante before any cards are dealt. The ante is money placed on the table in addition to the bets, and it is part of the pot going to the winner.

Antes vary according to the game and the casino and, most important, according to the stakes bet in the game. Sometimes an ante is small compared to the stakes, sometimes high. When a high ante is involved, the strategy of the game may change, for players may play aggressively with opening-round bets to "steal the ante," that is, force the other players out with large bets, just to win the antes.

In some Nevada casinos, the ante will be a normal one, for example, 50¢ in a $5–$10 game and $1 in a $10–$20 game. If the ante is higher, the game will attract more aggressive players. In some Nevada casinos, the ante is very low, sometimes as low as a quarter or nickel. This is done to attract more players. In those games, there's no point in stealing the ante because betting $10 to win $2 or $1 is fruitless and bad poker.

BETTING ROUNDS

In all forms of poker there are at least two rounds of betting, and sometimes several more. In draw poker, there is one round of betting before the draw and one after. In five-card stud there are four betting rounds; in seven-card stud there are five rounds; in Texas Hold 'Em, four rounds.

Most games have definite betting limits, though there can be no-limit games. Sometimes, more money can be bet in later betting rounds or when certain cards are showing than at the outset of play on the first round. For example, in a $5–$10 seven-card stud game in a Nevada casino, only $5 may be bet when no pairs are showing, or before the fourth round of betting. When a pair is showing in this game, the betting can begin at $10.

BETTING LIMITS

Poker is a money game, and can be played for any limit, from a penny all the way up to unlimited bets. Casino games generally run from $1 up, while private games are often played for quarters or dimes, depending upon the players and the type of poker that's being played.

The betting limits are generally two-tiered, with games played for $1–$2 or $5–$10, for example. In these games, particularly at stud poker, the higher limit is in force only when a pair is showing or in the later rounds of betting. And in the draw games, the higher limit is imposed after the draw, on the second round of betting.

The players usually set the rules concerning betting limits before play in private games, but sometimes these rules can be altered later on, as the game intensifies, losers drop out, and only the big winners remain.

Most games are played as table stakes games, particularly in casinos and clubs. This means that the player cannot bet more than he has on the table, in chips or cash. Sometimes a player has a bad losing streak, and, for instance, has only $10 left on the table in a $5–$10 game.

Even though this particular player may have more cash in his pockets, he can't reach for it while a game is going on, and after making one $10 wager, can't bet anymore, even though he has the best cards. The player, if he had been intelligent, would have put more money on the table before the game, so that he would have adequate funds to play and bet correctly.

When a player runs out of table stakes, his money is segregated in the pot, and all that the player bet, plus the other players' funds when that bet was made, is all the player can win. For example, if on the opening round, the player bet $5, was raised $5 and called, and then ran out of money, the money at that point is segregated. All subsequent bets made by other players can't be won by the player out of money, even though he had the best of all the hands. He can only win the segregated amount; the rest of the pot would be won by the second-best hand, the hand ranked highest among those players remaining in the game till the showdown.

BETTING METHODS

In stud games, in which the cards are dealt open (face up), the highest-ranking card shown opens the betting on the first round, or "brings it in." This is mandatory on the opening round.

For example, if only one player has an ace showing on the opening round, he must make the opening bet. He can't refuse to make the bet. In casino games, often the lowest-ranked card must open the betting on this round. But whatever the rule, high or low, the holder of that card must bring it in.

In high stud casino games, as we've pointed out, the lowest card opens the betting. This rule makes for more action, since it forces a bet from a player who might, as a matter of course, "fold his cards" and drop out of the game. In casino games, there's no option; the low card brings it in.

In draw poker, where betting is by sequence rather than by high card, since all cards are dealt closed (face down), a player may check or pass the betting if he is the first to bet, or in a game like jacks or better, if he doesn't have openers.

After a bet is made on any round of play, whether in stud or draw poker, the other players, in turn, have several options. First, they may "fold," that is, refuse to see (call) the bet. In that case, their cards are thrown to the dealer and removed from play. From then on, they're no longer involved with the betting action or play of the hand for that particular game.

The second option is "calling" the bet, that is, betting an amount equal to the original wager. The third option is "raising," that is, increasing the original bet. For example, on the first round of play in a $5–$10 draw poker game, if the original bet is $5, a player may increase that bet by $5, that is, raise the bet, by putting $10 into the pot. At this point, the second bettor has raised the first by $5. Now, when it is the original bettor's turn again, he must either call the bet or fold. He may reraise and then it will be up to the raiser to call the reraise or fold. Of course, the bet can be reraised again. Sometimes there's a limit to the number of raises allowed on any round of play. The usual casino practice is to limit the raises to three; unless only two players are in the game, then there are unlimited raises. No matter what rule is in effect concerning raises, all players in the game must have called or seen the last raise or bet before the next round of play begins.

After the first round of play, in either draw or stud poker, the first player to bet, either by turn or by holding the high cards (after the first round of high stud poker, the high hand bets first), may "check" without going out. Checking means passing one's hand temporarily, and a player who checks may again participate in the betting when it is his turn again.

After checking, all the player can do in most games is call the bet made, not raise it. This is a strict rule, and is enforced unless the game is "check and raise," as it is in many casinos. Then the original checker has the option of raising the bet made.

Of course, after a player checks, if a bet is made, he doesn't have to call it. The checker may then fold his cards when it is his turn again.

THE SHOWDOWN

After all the rounds of betting are over (the number of rounds depends on the type of poker played), if there are at least two players remaining there is the "showdown." At this point all the bets have been made. The player whose bet or raise was called last shows his cards first, then the other players show theirs in turn.

If the first player's cards are strong enough to win the pot, other players may simply fold their cards without displaying them to the remaining players in the game.

However, should the first player to show his cards not have the best hand, another player or players will show their cards, claiming the pot. After the various hands are examined, the highest-ranking hand will win the pot.

In the event of a tie, the pot will be split between the highest-ranking hands. For example, if three players remain at the showdown and one has three of a kind, but the other two have king-high straights, the pot will be divided equally between the holders of the straights.

In one variation of poker, high-low, the pot may be split equally between the highest hand and the lowest hand.

IRREGULARITIES IN POKER

We'll deal with the most common irregularities in poker, and the accepted rules concerning these irregularities. They'll generally apply to home or private games, since casino or club games will have their own rules for dealing with them.

When an irregularity calls for a misdeal, then all money in the pot prior to the misdeal is returned to the players. If no money had been placed in the pot prior to the discovery of the misdeal, the deal is void, and the cards are returned to the dealer and are not played or bet upon.

Incorrect Number of Cards in Deck

If the deck contains too many or too few cards, and this is discovered during the playing of a hand, that game is void, and all money previously bet is returned to the players. However, all previous games played with that same deck of cards are allowed to stand.

No Shuffle or Cut

If the cards were not shuffled or cut before being dealt, the game can be declared a misdeal by any participating player, but only before that player has placed his first bet.

Exposed Card During the Shuffle or Deal

There's a misdeal if any card is exposed during the shuffle or deal. The cards must be reshuffled. In draw poker, there is one exception to the rule. If the dealer exposes his own card, then there's no misdeal. He's forced to take his own exposed card.

Too Few Cards Dealt to A Player

If a player is dealt one card fewer than he should have, and this is found out prior to the betting, he may be given an additional card by the dealer, and then the game goes on, without a misdeal.

Once the betting has begun, however, it is a misdeal in draw poker. In stud poker, if the betting has begun, it's not a misdeal, but the player with too few cards has a dead hand and can't participate in the game.

In draw poker, if a player is dealt two fewer cards than he should have, the hand is a misdeal.

Too Many Cards Dealt to a Player

If a player has received too many cards in draw poker and has looked at his hand, it's a misdeal. In stud poker, if a player has looked at his hand after being dealt too many cards, his hand is dead; it's not a misdeal.

If a player in either draw or stud poker has received too many cards but hasn't looked at his hand, the extra card may be taken out of the player's hand by the dealer and put to one side, out of play for that game.

Skipping A Player

If the dealer skips a player during the deal, and it is pointed out before the betting begins, it's a misdeal. Once the betting has begun, it's no longer a misdeal, and the skipped player stays out of that game.

Exposing One's Own Card

Each player is responsible for his own cards, and there's no misdeal if he exposes his own card during the deal or play.

Dealer Exposing Final Card in Seven-Card Stud

If the dealer exposes the final card, there's no misdeal, but there can be no raises on this last round of betting.

Betting Out of Turn

If a player bets out of turn, the bet stands, and cannot be withdrawn. When it is his correct turn to bet, if the out-of-turn bet is sufficient, it stands as a call. If the bet is less than the previous bet, the player must equal the previous bet or forfeit the bet and his hand.

If the bet is greater than the previous bet, then it will be considered a raise.

Oral Bets

Any declaration made verbally, such as "I call," or "I raise," must then be honored. A player is bound by an oral statement of his intention to make a bet.

Checking Out of Turn

If a player checks out of turn, he is out of the game, unless no bets were made on that round of play.

Dropping Out or Folding Out of Turn

Once a player drops out of play, even if out of turn, his hand is now dead and he is out of the game, whether or not a bet has been made.

Dealer's Mistake in Calling Hand for Betting Purposes

If a dealer mistakenly calls out the wrong hand to bet first, and that hand opens the betting, any other player may point out this error. In that case, the opener's bet is returned and the correct opener has the option of betting.

Showdown: Mistaken Concession or Mistaken Dealer Statement as to Winner

If a player concedes the pot but it turns out that his hand is actually the winner, he may take the pot unless the winning player has already comingled the pot with his funds, or unless the player who conceded has already had his cards mingled with the discards.

If a dealer mistakenly states that a player has won the pot, his statement is not binding. In all cases at the showdown, the "cards speak for themselves," whether or not a player concedes or a dealer mistakenly states that the wrong player has won the pot.

However, if the second-best player has already mingled the pot funds with his own, or the winning player has mingled his cards with the discards, the win stands.

III

DRAW POKER— JACKS OR BETTER

In draw poker, all the player's cards are closed, that is, not exposed to the other players. In this game, also known as "jackpots," there are two betting rounds, one before and one after the draw. After the first betting round players may draw cards to improve their hands. These drawn cards are also unseen by the other players. The entire game is a closed one.

In draw poker the standard fifty-two-card deck is used, without jokers. The rank of the cards and the rank of the hands are as explained in Chapter One.

The pot can be won in two ways. The best hand wins at the showdown, or, if all other players have folded their cards, the one remaining player in the game can claim the pot.

Number of Players

Two to eight players can play draw poker; the best game is with six to eight players.

Antes

Antes are an important feature of draw poker, and whether the game is played at home or in a club or casino, an ante is required.

The amount of the ante may vary from game to game, but the norm is 10% of the highest bet allowed. Thus, in a $5–$10 game, the normal ante would be $1. Some players prefer higher antes, because they lead to more action and more aggressive play. A 20% ante, that is, 20% of the highest bet, would be a high ante. An ante less than 10% of the highest bet would be a small one.

Betting Limits

The limits must be agreed on before play begins, though they can be changed later with the agreement of the majority of the players. Usually the highest bet allowed is double the amount of the lowest bet. In this two-tier method of betting, the stakes can be $1–$2, $3–$6, $5–$10, and so forth.

When a game is played at $5–$10, for example, this means that the first round of play before the draw is limited to $5 bets and raises of $5. After the draw, the betting is in the $10 range, with increases of $10 for raises.

Therefore, when playing draw poker, the player must realize that the limits quoted for the game will be two-tiered, with the smaller bet allowed only before the draw, and the larger bet after it.

Openers

Draw poker, jackpots, is a unique game in that a minimum holding is required before a bet can be made. Since the player's hand is not exposed during the betting or the drawing of cards, once the game is over the opener may be required to show his hand to make sure that he had the minimum opening strength.

Should the opener fold during play, he is required to place his cards to one side, to be examined later to make certain that he did have opening values in his hand.

Jacks or better are required to open the betting. This means a pair of jacks, or any hand containing a higher-ranking pair or higher-ranking holdings, such as three of a kind, can open.

The Deal

After a dealer is chosen to start play (this can be done by drawing for the highest card, or by arbitrarily choosing someone to start the deal), the deal moves around in clockwise fashion, and each player has the chance to deal the cards.

After the dealer shuffles the cards, he gives them to the player on his right to cut. After they've been cut and restacked, the deal begins. But before commencing the deal, the dealer should make sure that each player has anted, and that the ante is correct. After this is done, the dealer will give out one card face down to each player in turn, commencing with the player to his left and going around clockwise until he gets the last card. Then he continues to deal one card face down at a time till all the players have five cards.

When this is done, he puts the stock of undealt cards to one side.

Play of the Game—First Round

The player to the dealer's left is in first and worst position, for he has to initiate the play, and thus give away his strength or lack of it before any of the other players has acted upon his hand.

He is "under the gun" in poker parlance. This player may check or make a bet. He can only make a bet if he holds the minimum required jacks or better. But even if he holds a valid opening hand, that player is not required to open. He might decide not to open because he feels that his opening cards are weak, or for strategic purposes, waiting to see what the others will do.

If this first position checks, it is up to the second-position player to bet. Then the third, and so forth, until a player bets. If any subsequent player makes the first bet, those who have checked before the bet are still in the game, and can call, but not raise the bet. Only players after the opener, who have not yet checked, can raise on this round.

After the opener bets, all those who check subsequent to this bet are out of the game. They have folded, since they didn't call the opener's bet. Their cards are given to the dealer face down, and put to one side in a discard pile.

After the opener bets and his bet is called by all players still in the game, or he is raised by one or more players and that raise is called by the players, the first round of play and betting is over.

The Draw

Now that the betting is over, each player may endeavor to improve his hand by discarding as many cards as he wishes from the hand he was dealt. Usually, not more than three cards are discarded in the draw. More may be discarded if the player so desires, but this is a weak move.

The player's discards are put to one side on the discard pile, and he is dealt the same number of cards from the top of the deck by the dealer.

If three cards are discarded, three more are dealt to the player by the dealer, so that the players always have five cards to form their hands.

Any player has the option of "standing pat," that is,

drawing no cards at all. Sometimes a player has a five-card holding such as a straight or flush and cannot break up his hand by drawing another card. Or he may be bluffing, or disguising the strength of his hand.

Sometimes, in a crowded game, with all players drawing cards, there will not be enough cards left in the stock to give each player sufficient cards. When that occurs, the players who can't get cards from the stock will put their cards to one side (not on the discard pile, so that they don't get their own discards back), and the discard pile will be shuffled and cards dealt to those players.

When cards are drawn, these cards are dealt at one time by the dealer. If a player wants two cards, two cards are dealt to him at one time (unlike the initial deal, in which players receive cards one at a time—one to the first player, then one to the second, and so on).

Second Betting Round

Now that each player has drawn cards, there is another betting round, begun by the opener. He may check or bet on this round, but a check doesn't remove him from play. Once a bet is made on this round of play, however, each player remaining in the game must call or raise the bet to remain in play. Anyone checking after a bet is made is deemed to have passed and folded his hand. Those cards are then returned to the dealer.

The dealer makes certain that all bets and raises have been called, and then will call for the showdown.

The Showdown

At this point, after the betting has been completed, the player who was called, or whose raise has been called, shows his hand. If another player has a higher-ranking hand, he will show that and claim the pot. If no one has a stronger hand the players may concede the pot without showing their hands.

The highest-ranking hand will win the pot at the showdown.

Showing Openers

If the opener hasn't shown his hand at the showdown, he must now show the openers; that is, the cards that opened the betting. After this is done, the cards are picked up by the next dealer to be shuffled, and a new deal will commence.

STRATEGIC PRINCIPLES IN DRAW POKER

There are two important concepts to be kept in mind in determining strategy. The first is the *ante*, and the second, *position*.

When the ante represents 10% or less of the maximum bet in the game, for example $1 in a $5–$10 game, that ante is considered normal or small. If the ante is 20% of the maximum bet, or $2 in a $5–$10 game, it's a high ante.

A high ante calls for more aggressive play. When the ante is normal or small, the strategy will be more cautious.

And this brings us to position. In a normal eight-man game, there will be eight positions. Number 8, the best position, is the dealer's spot. He acts and bets last. The worst is number 1, the spot just to the dealer's left. This player acts and bets first, which puts him at the mercy of later raises and draws.

In a low- or normal-ante game, the first four positions shouldn't open with less than a pair of aces. With two pair in those positions, the leading pair should be at least queens up, or in the fourth position, jacks up. In the fifth or sixth position, a pair of kings are sufficient to open, and in the seventh position, queens, or a pair of jacks with an ace. The dealer only should open with jacks.

In a high-ante game, where the ante is 20% of the maximum bet, the proper strategy is more aggressive. Here a player can open with kings or better in the first three positions. Queens are sufficient for the next three positions, and jacks or better for the final two positions.

If you study and learn this opening strategy, you'll be on your way to winning at draw poker. Most losers don't understand the importance of opening strategy, and will open the betting whenever they find themselves with a pair of jacks, no matter what position they're in.

This will lead to quick losses. Another bad move is to open with two small pair in the early positions (1–4). If you open with 9s and 5s, for example, in position 3, and you're raised, you will probably have to throw those two pair away. What else can you do? Suppose you call the raise, and the opponent takes two cards after you draw one. The odds are 11–1 against your improving, and you're probably facing three of a kind.

If your opponent now bets after the draw, after you pass with your two pair, to call his bet is to throw good money after bad. You've already made one bad bet, calling his raise.

Even if the raiser or caller has a pair of aces or kings only, he has a 2–1 chance of improving his hand, and if he improves, you're dead again. Be very careful with low-ranking two-pair hands, and never open them in early positions.

After learning the correct opening moves, you must gauge your opposition before determining whether to call or raise with your cards before the draw. If playing against a weak player who will open in early positions with jacks or queens, you can raise with aces and call with kings. But even if the opponent is weak, you must throw away your jacks and queens. These separate pairs are worthless even in late position against a previous caller. At best, you're equal to him in strength; at worst, he has a pair of aces already and you're dead.

If you have two low-ranking pair and a weak player has opened and another called, you can call. But you can't raise with these cards. If there are already three players in the game, all having made bets, throw your low-ranking two pair away, even in a late position.

If playing against stronger players, or players known as "rocks," because they'll only open with strong cards, you must alter your strategy. For example, if you know a player will only open with a pair of aces in early position, and with nothing less, you won't raise with a pair of aces, nor will you play any hand consisting of one pair only. What's the point? You want to have an advantage over the opener when you call or raise: If you are just even with him, get out.

Along with position, the number of players remaining in the game before the draw also counts heavily in determining strategy. Suppose you're in position 7, and the first five players check and position 6 opens the betting. You can eliminate the first five players because they don't have solid openers. You now have only one player to consider, other than the dealer.

If you have a pair of kings or aces here, you can raise, which accomplishes two things. One, you stop the dealer from trying to bluff by raising, or backing in with a weak pair where he might get lucky and outdraw you. You also force the opener to make a decision. If he opened with jacks because of position, he can't afford to see the raise. If he does, he's contributing money to a pot that should be yours.

Suppose the opener calls the raise after the dealer folds. He draws three cards. You draw three cards also. Chances are your kings or aces are stronger than his jacks or queens. If he checks after the draw, your bet will either drive him out or make him make another bad bet. You both have equal chances of improving your hands, but your hand will be higher than his if both of you make two pair.

If he bets after the draw, you can be sure he's improved. If you've improved, you can raise; if you haven't, get out. It's bad luck to be outdrawn, but that doesn't mean you have to make stupid bets or that you have to be stubborn.

What about four-flushes and open-ended straights? You can't open with these hands because they're not jacks or better, but what if you hold such a hand and someone else has opened? What do you do then?

First, looking at the chart on page 46 showing the probability of improving your hands by the draw, you'll see that the odds are approximately 4–1 against improving any open-ended straight or four-flush. Therefore, unless you're getting those odds out of the bets and the ante (that is, unless the ratio of the amount in the pot to the amount it would take to call is equal to or better than the odds against improving your hand—in this case 4–1), don't call with these hands.

Suppose you're the dealer in an eight-player game, and player 3 has opened and player 6 has called. It's a $5–$10 game, and there is a $2 ante. So, at this point, there's $16 in antes and $10 in bets for a total of $26. Your $5 bet will net you more than 5–1. You can bet here. But if the ante were only $1, there'd be only $18 in the pot, and your $5 bet would net you less than 4–1. In that instance, you can throw your four-flush or open-ended straight away. Play the odds and get value for your bets; otherwise stay out of the betting.

When you should raise the opener is another important strategic consideration. If you're holding trips, that is, three of a kind, and they're 10s or weaker, then you certainly want to raise the opener and try to get another bet out of him, while forcing those behind you to either fold or call your raise with weaker cards.

If you have three jacks or better, position and number of players will determine your move. Suppose you're holding three aces in position 6. After two checks, player 3 opens, players 4 and 5 fold and it's up to you. Your hand is very, very strong, so to encourage others to stay in the game, you could simply call here. Let's assume that the dealer also goes in, and now it's a three-way game. Player 3 draws two cards, you draw one card to disguise your strength, and the dealer draws three cards.

Player 3 now bets. He probably had trips to start or is saving a kicker with a high pair, worried about the two other players. His bet here suggests that he did have trips or has caught a pair to go along with his other high pair. At this point you can raise. The dealer behind you, if he's caught nothing, will fold. If he has caught trips, he will call. Player 3, the opener, will call.

Thus you'll make more than if you had raised on the first round. The dealer would probably have folded, and your raise would have been called by the opener. Then he'd check after the draw; you'd bet and he might fold if he had two pair.

With strength that should win even without improvement on the draw, you want to save your raising for the round after the draw, unless there are a couple of reraises before you. Then you can reraise. But otherwise, entice other players to bet, then hit them after the draw.

With low trips that can be outdrawn, you want to raise from the outset and get players out of the game. You want those small trips to hold up, and the fewer players in against you to draw, the better off you'll be.

Let us now summarize the strategy for draw poker, jack-pots.

1. In a low- or normal-ante game, the first four positions shouldn't open with less than aces. Two pair can also open, but the first three positions will require queens up. The fourth position can open with jacks up.

2. In the low- or normal-ante game, kings can open in the fifth or sixth position. Queens or a pair of jacks with an ace can open in the seventh position. Only the dealer should open with jacks.

3. In a high-ante game, kings are sufficient to open in the first three positions. Queens can open in positions 4–6, and jacks in the remaining positions.

4. Two small pair (10s or lower-ranked cards) should not be opened in positions 1–4. You can call with a weak two pair in a late position, but can't raise with them. But if there are at least three players in the game already, don't call with low-ranking two-pair hands.

5. Against strong or tight players, don't call with less than two pair, headed by at least a king. In very late position, however, seventh or dealer, you can call with two pair.

6. Against weak or average players, you can raise with a pair of kings or aces, if you are alone with the opener, and in fairly late position.

7. Don't raise with four-flushes or open-ended straights and only call if the pot yields better than 4–1 for your bet.

8. Raise with trips that are 10s or below, and call with jacks or higher when you hold three of a kind before the draw. With low trips you want to force players out; with high trips you want them to contribute to the pot.

9. Study the players you're up against and alter your strategy accordingly. Against strong or tight players, you need strong cards to raise when they open. Against weak players, who open with jacks or queens even under the gun, you can raise aggressively even when holding kings or aces.

10. Bluffing is not recommended, for good play and skill should win for you. But, if you must bluff, pick your spots only against strong players, after you've established that you play a strong game. A good player will respect your raise. Weak players are tough to bluff. They usually hang

45

on to their cards through raise and reraise. Don't attempt to bluff a weak player.

ODDS AGAINST IMPROVING DRAW POKER HANDS

Cards Held	Cards Drawn	Odds Against Improving
One Pair	3	2.5–1
Two Pair	1	10.8–1
Three of a Kind	2	8.7–1
Four-Flush	1	4.2–1
Open-Ended Straight	1	4.8–1
Inside or One-Sided Straight	1	10.8–1

In the next chart we'll examine the odds against improving specific hands by the draw.

Cards Held	Cards Drawn	Improving To	Odds Against
One Pair	3	Two Pair	5–1
		Three of a Kind	8–1
		Full House	97–1
One Pair with Ace Kicker	2	Aces Up	7.5–1
		Any Other Pair	17–1
		Three of a Kind	12–1
Two Pair	1	Full House	11–1
Three of a Kind	2	Full House	15.5–1
		Four of a Kind	22.5–1
Four-Card Straight Flush, Open-Ended	1	Any Improvement	2–1

46

CALIFORNIA CLUB POKER—JACKS OR BETTER

Chapter Eight, "California Poker Games," is devoted to the California club game. The rules of play, the ante structure and betting limits, and other general rules are covered in detail.

High poker, draw, is a popular game in these clubs. The major difference between the California club game and the ordinary private poker game is the use of a joker.

When a joker is used as the fifty-third card, it can only be used as an ace or to form flushes and straights. Thus it isn't truly a wild card, but a limited wild card.

If you care to play draw poker, high, jacks or better in the California clubs, first study the preceding sections of this chapter, then study Chapter Eight. At this point if you've mastered the strategies involved, you'll be ready to play any game of jacks or better anywhere.

Here are some basic changes that the joker makes in the odds against drawing hands. With the joker included, the odds against making a flush are 3.8–1, as against 4.2–1 in the standard game. The odds against making an open-ended straight are reduced to 4.3–1 from 4.8–1. Three aces will be a major factor in these games, because a joker can be converted into an ace.

With these figures in mind, you will see that aces become a much stronger hand in the club game, and the opportunities for drawing flushes and straights are increased quite a bit. Take this information into consideration when playing a club game.

There is a variation of jacks or better played in the California clubs called "open blind." Instead of requiring a hand of jacks or better to open, the first player, under the gun, to the dealer's left, must open the betting no matter what he has.

When involved in this game, you want to play much more aggressively. Therefore, when you hold an ordinary opening hand for jacks or better, in an open blind game, you can raise, rather than just call, because your hand becomes stronger. The later the position, the more aggressive you should be. If you're the dealer in an open blind game, you can raise with any pair plus a high card if no one else has called the opener.

When you are the opener in this game, even though you already have a bet in as the open blind, if you're raised, don't call unless you have aces and the raiser was in an early position. If the raiser was in a middle position, fourth through sixth, call with kings. You need only jacks to call a seventh-position raiser, and if you hold an ace, that's enough to call the dealer if he raised and you're head to head with him.

Since the joker can be converted into a second ace, in this situation, having been under the gun and forced to open, you can draw four cards and have a fighting chance against a dealer who raised. He's probably trying to steal the pot, and will be in a position to raise with any pair and any face card, such as jack, queen, king, or ace.

But always keep in mind the strength of your opposition, and adjust your play accordingly. Know who is weak and who is strong, who plays tight and who plays loose, and play accordingly, using our strategic guidelines.

IV

STUD POKER

Stud poker is the "open" version of poker, which means that some of the player's cards are seen by all the other participants in the game. Sometimes, in variations of stud poker, there are community cards, used by all the players to form their hands and seen by all the players.

The two most frequently played forms of stud poker are five- and seven-card stud. Five-card stud is rarely played in casinos, because only one card is hidden and four are shown, and there is little action in this game. However, seven-card stud, with three closed (face-down) cards and four open (face-up) cards, creates a lot of action because of the hidden values of the closed cards, and is a very popular game, both in private and in casino games.

FIVE-CARD STUD, HIGH

In five-card stud, the standard fifty-two-card deck is used, without jokers. The ranks of the cards and the hands are as explained in Chapter One, "The Basic Rules of Poker."

The pot can be won in two ways. The best hand wins at the showdown, or, if all the other players have folded their

49

cards, the one remaining player in the game can claim the pot.

Number of Players

Two to eight players can play five-card stud; the best game is one with six to eight players.

Antes

As a general rule, there is no ante in the private game, but there may be one in a casino game. I believe that it is a good rule to have an ante in any five-card stud game, because of the slowness of the action. Betting will be encouraged if a player can win the ante as well as the bets.

The normal ante is 10% of the highest bet, or $1 in a $5–$10 game. Any percentage lower than 10% would constitute a small ante; 20% would be a high ante.

Betting Limits

The limits must be agreed upon before play begins, though they may be changed later with the agreement of the majority of players. The betting range should be two-tiered, with the highest bet double the lowest bet, and no bets made between these limits. For example, if the lowest bet is $1 and the highest $2, a player can't bet $1.50.

The stakes are usually $1–$2, $3–$6, $5–$10, and so forth.

In private games, the lower bet will be in force until a pair is showing. Then the player can bet the lower or the higher amount, though the best rule is to enforce the higher amount only. For example, if the game is $5–$10, and a pair is showing, the minimum bet should be $10, without giving the player the option to wager $5 if he wishes. This makes for more action and a better game.

Even if no pair is showing, on the last two betting rounds the betting moves into the higher tier. In five-card stud there are four betting rounds. On the third and fourth rounds of betting, the wagers will be in the higher tier.

Betting Rounds

There are four betting rounds in five-card stud. At the outset of play, two cards are dealt to each player, one open and one closed. Then there is a betting round. After each of the remaining three cards are dealt there is another betting round. By the showdown, five cards will be in each player's hand, one closed and four open.

The Deal

Each player in a private game gets the deal in turn. The deal moves around the table clockwise. Unlike draw poker, in which the dealer has an advantage, since he acts and bets last, in five-card stud the rank of the cards determines the first bet on any round of play, and there is no advantage to dealing.

After the dealer shuffles the cards, he gives them to the player on his right to cut. After they've been cut and re-stacked, the deal begins.

If there's an ante in the game, the dealer should now make sure that it is correct. With no ante (the usual private game) he begins to deal the cards, giving one face down to the player on his left, and going around the table in that order, with each player getting a card face down. The dealer will get the last card. Then another card is dealt to each player in turn, face up. After each player holds two cards, one face up and one hidden or "in the hole," the dealer will place the stock to one side, and the first round of betting commences.

First Betting Round

In the standard private game of five-card stud, the highest card opens the betting on this round of play. It is a mandatory bet; the player cannot check or pass. After the holder of the highest card bets, then all players may act upon their hands in turn, beginning with the player to the opener's left. If two players have identical highest-ranked cards, the player closest to the dealer's left becomes the opener.

Each player, after the first bet is made, can fold his cards, call the bet, or raise the bet. After a bet is made, no player can check or pass his turn to bet. If he chooses to do this, his cards are folded, and he is out of play for that game.

After the round of betting is over, and the dealer determines this as well as making certain that each player has bet the correct amount, another card is dealt face up to the players remaining in the game. By this time, several of the players will have folded and their cards will be placed by the dealer in a separate discard pile, out of play for the rest of this particular game.

Second and Subsequent Betting Rounds

On the second round of betting, each player will have two cards face up and one in the hole, unseen by the other players. Now another round of betting commences, beginning with the player with the highest-ranking hand *seen* by all the players. Of course, the hole card isn't taken into consideration in determining the highest-ranking hand. It is the best hand "on board," seen by all the other players, that determines the opener.

On this round and on all future rounds of betting, the holder of the high hand doesn't have to open the betting. He may check and wait for another player to bet. If he checks, the player to his left now assumes the role of the opener, and he may either open the betting or check, and it thus goes around the table until one of the players opens the betting. If no one bets on this round, the entire round is checked, and another card will be dealt by the dealer.

However, should a player make an opening bet on this round, all players who have checked previously are still eligible to play and bet. Checking before an opening bet (on all rounds but the first, in which the high hand must open) doesn't eliminate one from the game.

Although players who checked before the opener may bet, they cannot raise. Only those players behind the opener, who haven't as yet checked, can raise the opener's bet. If a player checks, then finds the betting is opened, when it is his turn again, he may either call the bet and any subsequent raises or fold his cards. He cannot check twice.

On the third and all subsequent rounds of betting the same rules apply. The high hand has the option of opening the betting, but doesn't have to. However, if any player checks before the opening bet, his options are limited to calling or folding his cards.

The Showdown

After all four betting rounds are complete, and all bets have been made, there is the showdown, at which point, if two or more players remain in the game, the hands are shown to determine who has the highest-ranking one, and thus is the winner of the pot.

Suppose there are three players remaining in a game. The first player showed a pair of aces, the second a pair of queens and the third a pair of 7s. The first player opened with a $10 bet in a $5–$10 game, the second player called the bet, and the third player, with the 7s, raised the bet by $10 by putting $20 into the pot. Now the first player has the option of calling, reraising, or folding his cards. He calls the raise, as does the second player. Since the third player was called, he shows his cards first. His hand consists of 777K5. The first and second players, who had lower-ranking hands, don't have to show their cards, but concede the pot to the holder of the three 7s. However, if either of the two remaining players had a higher-ranking hand, such as three aces or three queens, he'd show his hand to claim the pot. By showing hands, we mean showing complete hands. The players already have four exposed cards; they'd have to show their hole card to make their entire card holding apparent to the other players.

STRATEGIC PRINCIPLES OF FIVE-CARD STUD, HIGH

There is only one unseen card in five-card stud, and thus most of the player's hand is apparent to the other players, with the exception, of course, of the single hole card. Still, that unseen card is an important one, for it can convert the cards on board into very strong hands.

For example, suppose a player holds ?5533 and another player, with his hole card (a king) apparent to us, is holding KQK8K. The second player has a very strong hand for five-card stud, three kings. However, he doesn't know the hole card of the other player. If it is a 5 or a 3, the other player will have a full house, and make the three kings a loser. Since the three kings is the opener on the final betting round, and faces only the 5s and 3s, he would be reluctant to open the betting. His open cards show that at best he can have three of a kind, not a full house, and if he opens the betting and is raised by the open 3s and 5s, he must either fold or put more money into a pot he knows is probably lost. That one unseen card thus can be a potent weapon.

The first thing to remember about five-card stud is that each player gets only five cards, and unlike draw poker, there's no opportunity to throw away weak cards and draw more cards to improve one's hand. Therefore, expect weak-ranking hands to win the pot in this game. A single pair is often strong enough to take the pot at the showdown.

Pairs can be categorized as weak, medium, and strong. Any pairs from 2s to 9s are weak pairs, 10s and jacks are medium pairs, and queens, kings, and aces are strong pairs, with kings and aces being very strong pairs. When aces show or are held by a player they are boss, and should be played accordingly, very aggressively.

What cards should a player stay in the pot with on the first round? Any pair will do, from 2s to aces. Even a weak pair can be improved to trips, or another pair added to it. Two pair is very, very strong in five-card stud.

However, whether a player will bet the pair depends upon circumstance and what is held by the other players, their strength as players and the way they bet their cards. For example, suppose you hold a pair of 4s on the opening round of play. You have the low card on board, and the game is opened by a king, who bets $5 in a $5–$10 game. Two players fold and the holder of a jack raises the bet to $10. All other players go out, and you, sitting to the right of the opener, now have to decide whether to call the raise. You know that the holder of the jack is an average player, so you try to gauge the meaning of his raise. He is holding either a pair of jacks or ace, jack. With any other holding he'd be insane to raise the king, unless he was bluffing. But why bluff at this stage of the game? There's no ante and only $5 in the pot to win with the raise. With ace, jack, or two jacks, your 4s are rather weak, and still the king has to bet behind you.

The best policy is to fold. You're in bad position, and may already be second, and possibly third, in high-ranking hands.

Weak hands, that is, weak pairs, can be played, but not against opening raises. Even medium pairs should be thrown away on opening-round raises. There's an outside chance you may have been bluffed out, but on the other hand, what's the point of contributing to the pot round after round, raise after raise, when you may be dead from the outset of play? That's not good poker.

Only a holding of queens, kings, or aces is solid enough to withstand opening raises. And these cards are good enough to reraise. Suppose, in the same game we mentioned, the king had opened, the jack raised, but you were holding queens. Now, we have an altogether different situation. After the jack raises, there's only the king behind you. You can reraise here.

Which brings us to the next strategic situation. On the opening round, you want to have a chance to win the pot. If you don't have that chance, you might as well throw away your cards. If the high card on board is a king, and all you have is a queen, dump it. A king against an ace is worthless. If you have a chance of pairing, so does he. If neither of you pair, you're beaten on any round.

And the same advice goes for subsequent rounds of betting. Once you see you've been beaten, get out. For example, if you hold a pair of kings, and on the opening round, you see two separate aces, and both stay in, here's a good opportunity to raise. On the next round you draw an ace, and neither ace improves, but both check to you, then call. On the third round of play, one of them catches an ace, and now suddenly you're not top dog anymore. The aces come out swinging and it's time for you to fold. Forget about what you have in the pot up to this time. That's lost, and don't throw away two more bets just because you've already made two bets. You're beaten on the board, and even if you make two pair, the aces may already hold two pair. Fold those cards. Don't fight better hands with expectations, unless the odds are there, in your favor.

Expections are slight, not great, in five-card stud. You're only going to get five cards. You have to play tightly, with the expectation, not of improving, but of folding hand after hand, waiting for a situation in which you're the top man, or have a disguised hand that gives you a solid chance to win.

That's why this game is rarely played in a casino and is in great decline as a private game, having been overtaken by seven-card stud in popularity. Good players usually play a tight game of poker, but at the same time, they want to get in there swinging when they can really disguise a hand and then take the pot at the end. Both situations make for dull play in five-card stud. If you're in against good players, there'll be little action hand after hand, as everyone folds.

And if a good player stays in with you with cards that seem inferior, you can be sure he's trying to trap you. The easiest thing in this game is to just fold your cards. That's why I recommend an ante. The game is too slow otherwise. At least, with an ante, and preferably a high one, 20% of the highest bet, there will be a lot of opening-round action trying to steal that ante.

Finally, if you do have solid winning cards and there are a few players who are chasing your superior hand, make them pay dearly for this privilege. You'll be able to spot the weak players soon after play begins. They're the ones going in with second-best hands, hoping for miracles. Make them pay for their lack of skill.

Let's now summarize the strategy for five-card stud, high.

1. The only cards to stay in with on the opening round are pairs or a card higher than the high card on board. Otherwise fold.

2. If raised on the opening round by an opponent who holds a higher card than your pair, fold your cards. Don't chase superior cards.

3. If you are raised by an opponent who holds a weaker-ranked card than your pair, reraise immediately on the first round of betting.

4. If you're not holding a pair, get out if any card on the board is higher than your highest card.

5. If on any subsequent round you realize you're

beaten, get out. Don't throw good money after bad. The money you've put into the pot isn't yours anymore, it's the pot's.

6. Don't play for flushes and straights in five-card stud. They are very difficult to make and an odd card on any betting round will destroy your hand. Go for these hands only if you have an "out," that is, an ace leading the suit or straight, so that, even if you don't make the flush or straight, pairing the ace will give you a winning hand.

7. Play tightly. It's the only way to win at this game.

8. Study your opponents. You must be aware at all times who is weak and who is strong. Respect strong players and the cards they hold. Punish the weak players.

9. If one or more players is chasing your hand, which is strongest, make them pay for this privilege. Make maximum bets, or if they lead with a bet, raise them.

10. Try to play with a high ante if this is the only game in town. This will lead to more action.

SEVEN-CARD STUD, HIGH

Seven-card stud has become the most popular of all the stud games, and with good reason. There are three hidden cards, two dealt at the beginning of play and the third dealt last. Only four of the seven cards are seen by all players, and all kinds of strong hands can be hidden as a result.

There are also five rounds of betting, which brings much more action than five-card stud. This is an ideal game to learn, because not only is it a popular one, but there's also money to be made, since many weak players prefer seven-card stud, thinking that it's merely a game of luck. The astute and skillful player will therefore have a good opportunity to win against these players.

In seven-card stud, the standard fifty-two-card deck is used, without jokers. The ranks of the cards and the hands are as explained in Chapter One.

The pot can be won in two ways. The best hand wins at the showdown, or, if all the players have folded but one, that one remaining player can claim the pot.

Number of Players

Two to eight players can play seven-card stud; the best game is one with six to eight players.

Antes

There is usually no ante in a private game, because there's enough action here without an ante. In the casino game, the ante is usually 10% of the *minimum* bet in the game; therefore, in a $5–$10 game, the ante would be 50¢.

Betting Limits

The limits are usually agreed upon before play begins, though, later on, if several players drop out, the remaining players, who are usually the big winners, may decide to increase the limits.

The betting limits are two-tiered, with the higher limit double the lower limit. Thus games may be 25¢–50¢, $1–$2, $5–$10, and so forth. No bets can be made between the two amounts. Thus, in a $5–$10 game, there can be no bets of $6 or $7, for example.

In private games, the lower limit remains in force as the basic bet until a pair is showing or until the fourth round of betting begins. The betting is then at the higher limit.

Betting Rounds

There are five betting rounds in seven-card stud. At the outset of play, three cards are dealt to each player, two down and one up. Then there is a betting round. After each of the remaining cards, four in all, are dealt, there's another betting round. The final betting round, the fifth, comes after the seventh card is dealt. This card is dealt face down. By the showdown, each of the players remaining in the game will have seven cards, three face down and four face up.

The Deal

Each player in a private game gets the deal in turn. The deal moves around the table clockwise. The dealer has several duties, among them dealing the cards one at a time in correct order and making certain that the pot is correct (that is, that all players have put in the right amount of money or chips). He must also determine who has the high hand on the board, and therefore, who is the first player to open the betting on each round.

After the dealer shuffles the cards, they are given to the player on his right to cut. After the cut is made and the cards restacked, the deal begins.

The first player to get a card is the player to the dealer's left, and a card is dealt face down to him and to each player in turn, with the dealer getting the final card. Then a second card is dealt face down in the same manner. After each player has received two cards face down, a third card is dealt face up, seen by all the other players in the game.

After each player has thus received three cards, two face down and one face up, the dealer puts the stock of cards to one side, and the first round of betting commences.

First Betting Round

The high card will open the first round of betting in private games. This is a mandatory bet, and must be made by the holder of that highest-ranking card. If two players hold identical highest-ranking cards, the player closest to the dealer's left, the first one to get that card, opens the betting.

After the opening best is made, each player in turn, beginning with the player to the opener's left, can either call the bet, raise the bet, or fold his cards. After a bet is made, no player can check his hand; doing this means he is out of the game and must fold his cards.

After all bets have been made on this round, the dealer collects the discards of those players who have folded and puts them to one side before dealing cards for the second round of play.

Second and Subsequent Betting Rounds

Each player will receive another card from the dealer, face up, before the second round of betting. At this point, those players remaining in the game, that is, those players who haven't folded their cards in the first round of play, will each have four cards, two face up and two unseen by the other players.

The highest-ranking hand will bet first. If two players have identical highest-ranking hands, the player closest to the dealer's left will have the option of betting first.

The holder of the highest-ranking hand may bet or check. If no pairs are showing, then he will make the minimum bet. If pairs are showing and he has the highest pair, he must bet the maximum wager.

However, the holder of the high hand doesn't have to bet. He can check his hand. This doesn't eliminate him from the game, for he has the option of calling any opening bet and subsequent raises, if any.

If this player bets, each player in turn, beginning with the player on his left, must call the bet, raise, or fold the cards they're holding. If a player raises, all other players in that round must see the raise in order to stay in the game. For example, if the opener has a pair showing and bets $10 in a $5–$10 game, another player calls, and two other players fold before a raiser who makes it $20, all players behind the raiser must either call the raise or fold their cards. Of course, they can reraise as well, up to $30, in which case all the players behind the reraiser must put in money to see the $30 reraise.

For example, if player A bet $10, B called with $10, C raised to $20, and D raised to $30, then A must bet $20 more, B must bet $20 more, and C $10 more to call the reraise. Of course, if they're inclined, any of these players, A, B, or C, could have reraised to $40, and then the other players would have to call the reraise or fold.

On the third through the last rounds of betting the same rules apply. Since the last card is dealt face down, the high hand on the fourth round of betting is also the high hand on the last round of betting.

Professionals refer to rounds of betting in a different manner. The number of cards held by the player is the number of "Streets." The opening betting round, since each player holds three cards, is known as "Third Street." When four cards are held, it's "Fourth Street," and so forth to the last round of betting, which is known as "Seventh Street" or "down the river." Many amateurs don't know these "Street" names for betting rounds, however.

The Showdown

After all five betting rounds are complete, and all the bets are in the pot, if two or more players remain in the game, there's a showdown, with the players, beginning with the player whose last bet was called, or the last raiser to be called, showing his cards first, all his cards.

Note that each player has been dealt seven cards. Therefore, since poker hands are formed from only five cards, the five cards that make up the highest-ranking hand the player has are the only ones counted.

Suppose a player holds 9(H), 9(S), 9(C), 8(H), 7(H), 4(H), and 3(H), at the showdown. Although the player has three of a kind, the three 9s, he also has a heart flush. And since a heart flush is the higher-ranking of the hands, that's what he'll declare.

Some players, after one player puts down his cards, concede without showing their cards, which is permissible. However, often it's best, if you're a beginner, to show all your cards, for the cards "speak for themselves." For example, suppose you held the above hand and thought your best hand was only three 9s. If one of the players showing his hand held three queens and claimed the pot, and you showed all your cards, even if you said "I have three 9s" the cards would speak for themselves, and no matter what you said, it is apparent that you have a heart flush. The dealer's duty at this time is to point out your flush and announce that you're the winner of the pot. But the dealer can't do this if you concede without showing your hand.

Seven-card stud is the first card game we've discussed in which the players hold more than five cards. Therefore, a player must be careful to examine all seven cards to make sure that he is aware of the highest-ranking hand to be made from those seven cards.

Even professionals sometimes slip up. It's not that they're stupid or unskilled. After many hours of card playing, even the best of us get weary, our eyes blur, and we make mistakes. Therefore, when in doubt, display the cards and let them speak for themselves.

STRATEGIC PRINCIPLES OF SEVEN-CARD STUD, HIGH

The first strategic consideration we face is which hands to stay in with before the first betting round. The choice is broader here than in a game like five-card stud, where our hand is formed by only five cards. We have seven cards to choose from to form our best hand, and therefore we can stay in the first round even if we seem to be beaten on the board.

The best hand at this point, of course, is trips, or three of a kind. Any trips are strong, and should win the pot for us, either alone or improved into a full house. So, no matter how low the trips are, whether three 2s or 3s, we're in that pot to stay to the end. Of course, the higher the trips, the stronger the hand, in case another player has trips also. But no matter how high or low the three of a kind is, it will be beaten by a flush or straight if the hand doesn't improve. Those are the two hands that will beat us in this situation. We're disregarding other hands, such as straight flushes and so forth, because they rarely occur, and don't have to be taken into consideration. If a player makes this kind of monster hand, God bless him, he deserves to win.

With a holding of trips, we want as many players to stay in the game as possible, improving their hands to two pairs and possible straights and flushes, so we don't raise at all on the opening round, even if others have raised the pot. Let them all fight it out; we want to disguise the strength of our hand. On Fourth Street we don't raise, still keeping as many players as possible in contention, to feed the pot and build it up for us.

Only on Fifth Street do we swing into action. A raise here only further disguises our hand, because the players will assume the last card or two they see caused us to raise, and these cards will have no relevance to our initial strength.

For example, suppose you start off with 888. On the opening round, there was a raise by an ace, and this was called by you and three other players. At this point the hands look like this: (* = hidden card)

Player A holds **10
Player B holds **A
Player C holds **J

You hold 888

On the next round of play, the hands look like this:

Player A holds **1010

Player B holds **A6

Player C holds **J(D)5(D)

You hold 8885

Player A opens the betting with his 10s; the ace hand belonging to Player B raises, Player C, you, and Player A call the raise.

On Fifth Street, the hands look like this:

Player A holds **10104

Player B holds **A69

Player C **J(D)5(D)A(H)

You hold 88859

Player A checks his 10s, showing that he has at best two pair, for if he had three-of-a-kind, there'd be no reason for him to check. Player B bets, Player C calls, and you raise. Player A folds the 10s. Player B now hesitates and looks over your hand. He figures you for a possible straight, for he's a weak player himself, and thinks possible straights and flushes can raise. He calls your raise, and Player C does also, with his four diamond holding.

On Sixth Street, the hands look like this:

Player B holds **A6910

Player C holds **J(D)5(D)A(H)3(D)

You hold 888595

You are high with the 5s and bet. Player B has two pair headed by the aces, and calls. Player C with his third diamond has made his flush and raises. Now you reraise. Player B is baffled. How could you bet into a flush with only a straight, or maybe two small pair?

Player B looks at his hole cards. He has an ace and 9 in the hole, but one ace and 9 are on board. His chances of getting that full house are slim, but he's gone in so far, and there's always hope, so he calls your reraise.

The diamond flush has it already made, but now he's

worried about a hidden full house somewhere, so he calls your reraise, and now the last card is dealt.

Players B and C still have the same cards showing on Seventh Street, when you open the betting again. Player B hasn't improved, hems and haws and throws away his cards, wondering whether he's been bluffed out of a pot. He can't figure your bet.

Player C calls; you show your full house and get the pot.

The other players had been baffled by your "slow play." If you "fast played" it, that is, came out raising right from Third Street, they'd realize that the 8 was the key card, and that you weren't going for a low straight. If you'd have raised the ace right off, the other players would have gone out, and the ace might have gone out on the next round if he didn't improve, if you raised again.

Trips must be played this way; slow at first and then aggressively from Fifth Street on. They should win by themselves or improve to a full house and then win, but occasionally there'll be no improvement and someone will back in with a flush or straight and beat the trips. This can happen, of course, but in the long run these trips will make a lot of money for you if you slow play them on Third and Fourth Street and let the other players stay in to build up a big pot.

After trips, let's look at pairs. The best kind of pair is a concealed one. For example, it's much better to have KK4 with the kings concealed as hole cards than to have the kings split so that one of the kings is an open card.

With high pairs, and in seven-card stud we consider 10s or higher-ranked cards high pairs, it's best that both of the cards that form the pair be concealed. If they're split, one of these strong cards is apparent to the other players, and your options are more limited.

When you hold a high pair, either concealed or split, you should raise on the opening round if you can, in order to force other players out. You want to win the pot and limit the competition. For example, suppose you're in the third position in an eight-player game and are holding KK4, with the 4 showing as the open card. The player in the first position has a queen and is high on the board. He opens the betting, the second player, with a 10, calls, and now it's up to you. Raise, especially since there are five players behind you. Your raise will force many of these players out. Normally, if there is no raise, a couple of them might "limp in" just by calling the original bet. And limping in may enable them to draw a card on Fourth Street that makes their hands stronger than yours, or potentially stronger. Get them out right away.

With 10s or higher at the outset, play aggressively and raise the pot, unless it's been raised by another player before you whose open or "door card" is higher than your pair. For example, if you hold 10s and a queen opened the betting, but was raised by a jack, you have to feel that the holder of the jack has jacks. Fold here.

But if your "kicker" or third card with the 10s is a king or ace, you can call the raise, with the expectation of pairing the king or ace.

Aggressive play with good pairs, from 10s on up, is important. It gives you control of the game and eliminates players who might go along for the ride, trying to stay in with just a low bet.

When you hold weak pairs, that is, pairs from 2s to 9s, you can stay in, but you can't take an opening raise unless your kicker is higher than the raised card. For example, you hold 474 and the pot is raised by a queen. You fold. The queens are much stronger than your pair of 4s. However, should your kicker be an ace or king, you can stay in.

Don't stay in with cards that aren't strong enough to win the pot later on. Your pair of 4s won't beat queens if your kicker is lower than the queen. There are plenty of opportunities to play hands in seven-card stud. Play only those hands that give you control at the outset, that are top dog on the table, or have the potential, with one draw, to win the pot.

Now we come to three-flushes and three-straights. These are hands that we will stay in with, with one exception, which we'll get to later. Three-flushes and three-straights are drawing hands, unlike the other hands we've already discussed. If we don't draw well, we have a losing hand.

The best kind of three-flush or three-straight is one headed by a high card, such as a king or queen. Thus, we have a chance not only for a flush, for example, but also for a high pair. This is giving ourselves an "out," another way to win the pot.

For example, a flush of K95 is much, much stronger than one of 974. We may pair the king with the first three-flush and have another way to win the pot. Even if we pair the 9 in the second hand of 974 we have nothing on Fourth Street. If players are in the game, we can be sure that one of them has at least a pair of 10s by now, or the potential to pair a high card. We'll just be contributing money to the pot, and if we don't get our fourth card to the flush on Fourth Street, we're a very long shot to get a flush.

With a weak flush or straight, one headed by a card lower than a 10, it doesn't pay to stay in on Third Street if there's a raise. Get out at that time. If you hold at least a 10 you can stay in and hope to improve on Fourth Street. However, suppose that holding a 1086 of hearts, you buy a jack of spades on Fourth Street. Get out. There's nothing left to play for.

Stay in with a high straight or high flush through Fourth Street, if two of the cards are really high, such as king, queen, jack as a potential straight, or ace, queen, 5 of spades. Even if you buy an odd card in these situations, you still have the chance of making a hand if you pair any of the high cards.

But with only one high card, if you don't improve and

make a four-straight or four-flush on Fourth Street, get out of the game.

What if you do make a four-straight or four-flush with the first four cards dealt? Do you raise? The answer is no. Even with the first four cards matching as a flush or a straight, the odds of drawing either a flush or a straight (as separate hands) are below 50%. You have a 47% chance of converting the flush and only a 43% chance of making the straight in this situation.

Thus, a four-flush is an underdog against a pair of aces. Not many people know this, and poker players think that a four-flush or four-straight with three cards to draw is a big favorite to win a pot against the holder of a pair higher than the highest card in the flush. It just isn't so, and those weak players who constantly raise these hands end up losing a lot of money.

When you do have a four-flush or four-straight, you must avoid raising. You intend to go to Seventh Street with these hands, so just call the bets, and hope to draw that fifth to the straight or flush. When you do, you will be a big favorite to win the pot. But be patient. Raising on expectations will destroy your bankroll at the poker table.

After you've decided to stay in, if you hold drawing cards, you can't raise on the come, that is, on expectations. You must wait till you make that flush or straight. If you hold a pair of high cards, you must play them aggressively to drive out the other players. With three of a kind, you want to keep the other players in the game, so you play them slow, waiting for Fifth Street to begin raising.

Don't be a "calling station." That's the term the experts use for players who merely call bets hand after hand. If your hand is good enough to call, it should be good enough to raise. If not, then fold the cards. Of course, there are a few exceptions to this rule, notably when you're playing for a straight or flush.

But otherwise, with solid cards, but cards that, by themselves, can't win, such as a pair of kings or aces, you must raise and get the other players out before they draw cards to beat your hand. If they stay in, then punish them; make them pay more money to draw against you. If you have a high pair, kings or aces, and another player is going for a flush or straight, make him pay. Raise him. He's an under-dog against you, and must draw to beat you. Make him pay for this privilege.

If you don't play aggressively, you're going to get players in cheaply or for free to beat you. Every time a hand is passed, you can be sure there's one weak player, and often more, in that game. There's never any reason to give play-ers a free card if you're the high man. Going in with the solid cards we have mentioned gives you the chance to win every pot you've put money into. Don't be a small winner; win the big pots by betting aggressively.

Let's now summarize the strategy for seven-card stud, high.

1. When you're dealt trips at the outset, slow play them till Fifth Street, then come out raising. Don't raise at the outset. You want to get as many players in the game as possible to improve their hands and contribute to the pot.

2. With a high pair, 10s or higher, raise from the outset to drive out the other players. But if these cards, such as 10s, are apparently not the best pair, get out. For example, if a jack raises a queen opener, get out with your 10s.

3. If you hold a medium pair, with an even higher kicker, such as a king or ace, you can call a raise by a jack or queen with the expectation of pairing the king or ace. But just call here; don't raise on drawing hands, hands that need help to win the pot.

4. With a pair of 9s or below, you can stay in on Third Street, but can't afford to take a raise, unless your kicker is higher than the raised card you see.

5. Stay in with three-flushes and three-straights before the first betting round, but if there is a raise make sure that

your straight or flush is headed by at least a 10. The higher the high card in your flush or straight at the outset, the better your hand is.

6. If you have only one high card in the flush or straight and don't improve on Fourth Street, then fold the cards. If you have two high cards you can stay in, for you have a couple of outs with the ace and king, or king and queen, you're holding.

7. Don't raise, even with a four-flush or four-straight with the first four cards you're holding. You're still an underdog against a high pair with either of these hands, and you don't want to raise with drawing cards.

8. After you've gotten the straight or flush, then raise. Make the pots as big as possible when you have the winning hand going into Seventh Street.

9. Play aggressively in seven-card stud. When you have a high pair raise at the outset to get the other players out, then raise against players who only have drawing possibilities, such as four-straights or four-flushes. You're the favorite; make them pay for the privilege of staying in.

10. Don't be a "calling station." If your hand is good enough to play, unless it's a drawing hand, it should be good enough to raise. Don't give the other players free rides or cheap rides by not raising. Make those pots big, because you're going to be winning most of them if you stay in with the cards we recommend.

V

LOWBALL POKER

Lowball, or loball as it's called in the casinos of Nevada and California, is a game that can be played, just as high poker is, as either draw or stud poker.

Lowball is just what the name implies—the low hand wins the pot, rather than the high hand.

In lowball poker, straights and flushes are not counted. Having a flush or straight doesn't penalize the low holder; it is not taken into consideration in valuing the hand. Thus, the best hand in lowball, 5432A, is merely a "54" hand, which beats all low hands in lowball. The fact that it is also a straight, as we've mentioned, is irrelevant in valuing the hand.

In lowball, the hand is valued by calling out the first two cards, the highest-ranking cards, that is. Thus, a 7543A would be known as a "75" hand, and that would be lower and thus beat a "76" hand, consisting of 7632A.

The ace is always counted as a 1 in lowball, and is the best card to hold. If a player held KQJ10A, of course a terrible hand in lowball, it would be counted as a "king-queen" hand, with the ace counted as the low card in this holding.

Ranking of the Hands in Lowball

In lowball, the highest card of the five-card holding, or the five-card holding the player chooses to represent his hand in the seven-card versions, sets the parameters of the hand. The lowest of the high cards determines the winner. Thus, if there's a showdown between a Q542A and a J9854, the jack hand wins, even though the other four cards in the queen-high hand are lower.

If both high cards are identical, then the players announce their next-highest card and so forth till a winner is chosen. A hand of 9754A will beat a hand of 97542, because the ace is lower than the deuce in the second hand.

Here are the best possible hands in lowball, in ascending order.

The best of all lowball hands is 5432A, called a "wheel" or "bicycle" in poker slang. No hand can beat this, and only an identical holding can tie it, in which case the pot would be split.

The second-best hand is 6432A, third-best is 6532A, and the fourth-best hand is 6542A.

The above hands are true premium hands and are rarely seen in lowball. It is not necessary to memorize which hand is best, second-best, and so forth. When hands are put out on the showdown, it will be obvious by the call of the first two cards. If one player has 65, he will lose to a 64 hand, and all hands led by a 6 will beat all hands led by a 7 or a higher card.

Thus far we've examined hands that contain five unmatched cards. But sometimes players will hold pairs when placing their cards down at the showdown. In this case, the lowest-ranking pair bests all higher-ranking pairs. The aces are the lowest-ranking of all pairs; they're equivalent to 1s. Then come 2s, 3s, and so forth, all the way up to kings, which are the highest-ranking of all pairs and thus losers to any other holdings of one pair.

If the pairs are identical, the odd cards are examined and the lowest-ranking of the high odd cards wins. QQ543 beats QQ63A. Here the 5 is lower than the 6.

When players hold even higher-ranked cards, such as two pair and so forth, reverse the rank order for high poker to determine the winner. A two-pair hand will beat three of a kind and so forth, but this will rarely happen in lowball. There's no point in staying in the game with either of these hands, as you cannot expect to win a pot in lowball poker with such cards.

LOWBALL, DRAW POKER

The standard fifty-two-card deck is used, without jokers. The ranks of the cards and the hands are as explained in the beginning of this chapter.

The pot can be won in two ways. The best hand wins at the showdown, or, if all the players have withdrawn from play except one, that remaining player can claim the pot.

Number of Players

Two to eight players can play lowball, draw poker; the best game is one with six to eight players.

Antes

There is normally an ante in all draw games, and lowball is no exception. A normal ante would be 10% of the highest bet; a low ante would be anything less than this percentage, and a high ante would be 20% of the highest bet.

Blind Bets

Sometimes, and normally in the casino game, this game is played with a blind bettor. The player to the left of the dealer, the first one to bet, must open the betting regardless of his holdings. Thus he is the "blind" bettor. If there is a blind bettor, it usually is a "live blind," which means that, when the others in the game on this first betting round have called his opening bet, he can come back and raise it. For example, suppose player A opened blindly in a $5–$10 game with a $5 bet. Players C and E called, with all other players folding. Now player A can raise the bet to $10 on this round of play and players C and E will have to see the raise or fold their cards.

However, the usual game of lowball, when played privately, doesn't call for a blind bet.

Betting Limits

The limits are two-tiered, with the higher bet usually double the lower bet. The game can be $1–$2, $3–$6, $5-$10, $10–$20, and so forth.

The lower betting limit is in force during the first round of play, before the draw. After the draw, the betting is at the higher limit.

Betting Rounds

There are two betting rounds. After each player has received five cards, the player closest to the dealer's left has the option of opening (when there is no blind) and if he passes, the player to his left has that option, and so on clockwise around the table. After a bet is made by the opener, any player who hasn't already bet can fold, call the bet, or raise. Any player who passed before the opening bet cannot raise, unless check and raise is agreed upon before the game.

After the bets on the opening round have been made, each player remaining in the game may draw cards to improve his hand, discarding the same number of cards. Once all the players have drawn cards, there's a second round of betting at the higher limit. After this is completed, there is a showdown, with the lowest hand winning.

The Deal

Each player gets the deal in turn. In draw poker, the dealer always has an advantage, since he bets and acts upon his cards last.

The dealer must shuffle the cards, then give them to the player on his right to cut. After they've been cut and restacked, he deals the cards one at a time, face down, beginning with the player to his left and continuing around the table until he, the dealer, gets a card. This is repeated till each player has five cards, all dealt face down.

The dealer should make certain that the ante is correct before the deal, and that all the bets are correct before the draw. Then he should be certain that he deals the correct number of cards to each player during the draw, and that the bets are correct before the showdown.

All cards discarded by players who fold or who drew cards to their hand must be put to one side in a discard pile by the dealer and not touched again during the play of the game.

First Betting Round

Since this is lowball, there is no set rule about opening, as there is in high draw poker, where a pair of jacks or better is necessary to open the betting.

Here the betting commences with the player to the dealer's left, who has the option of opening the betting or passing. If he passes, he's not out of the game; he can come back and call a bet or raise when it is his turn again.

Each player can pass or open the betting in turn. When a player opens, he must open at the lower of the two betting amounts; if it's a $5–$10 game, he opens for $5. Then players who haven't previously passed must call the bet or raise in order to stay in the game. After a pot is opened, there can be no checks.

Those players who previously passed can only call; they cannot raise on this round of play. After all the bets are in, and are correct, there is a draw and a second betting round.

The Draw and Second Betting Round

Each player draws cards in turn, and the player taking cards must discard the same number of cards he wishes to draw. These discarded cards are put to one side by the dealer, who then deals the same number of cards to the player, so that each hand contains five cards.

After each player has been given his cards, the second round of betting begins. On the draw, a player may take as many cards as he desires; in draw poker, lowball, rarely will any player take more than two cards. Some players may wish to "stand pat"; a player doesn't have to take any cards if he feels his hand is strong enough to win without drawing cards to it.

The betting begins with the opener of the first round of betting starting the action. He can pass or check, or make an opening bet on this round, betting the higher limit of the betting range. If it's a $5–$10 game, he'd have to open, if he cared to, with a $10 bet.

If players pass on this round, they're still in the game until another player opens the betting, for they may call the bet when it's their turn to play. But they can only call; they can't raise, since they checked originally.

The Showdown

After all the bets are made on this second round of betting, if there are two or more players remaining in the game, there's a showdown. The player who was called shows his cards first; then the other players can show their cards to claim the pot or concede the pot without showing their cards.

For example, suppose the player who was called, Player B, shows his hand, which consists of 86432. There are two other players in the game. Player C concedes, but Player D shows his hand, 8542A, and claims the pot, since he has 85, compared to Player B's 86. Player D wins the pot.

STRATEGIC PRINCIPLES OF LOWBALL, DRAW POKER

Since the game is draw, we have to take into consideration our position at the table and the type of ante involved. First, the ante. In a low-ante game, we want to play conservatively, because the ante won't mean that much. The same consideration holds true for a normal ante. But when there's a high ante (20% of the highest bet) we must play more aggressively, because if we can steal that ante, it's very worthwhile.

Then there's position. Obviously the later the position, the more benefit it is to us, because we can see what the other players are doing before we make any decision. And if another player has opened the betting, we can raise if our strategy calls for this move. If we open the betting, we leave ourselves open to the other players.

Now position isn't constant. Sometimes we'll be in early position, sometimes in later position. By early position we mean the first four places in an eight-man game. Late positions are the sixth, seventh, and eighth seats on any round of play. The fifth position is in between and should be played a little looser than the first four positions and a little tighter than the late positions.

The best hands to have are pat hands, but at no time do we want to play a hand headed by a jack, queen, or king,

78

even if it's pat, and even if we're in last position.

In seventh or eighth position we can bet and open play with a 10-high hand. In the fourth, fifth, or sixth position we can open with a 9-high pat hand, and in the first three positions it would have to be at least an 8-high hand.

When drawing one card, and we never want to draw more than one card, we should have a 7-high hand in the first four positions to open, an 8-high in the fifth and sixth positions, and a 9-high in the seventh position. Only in the last position can we open with a four-card hand headed by a 10.

Remember these sequences; they're of utmost importance in playing lowball draw. We're out to win the pot, not contribute to it, and not to bet just because, though our cards are awful, we have a hunch that we're going to draw two good cards. The odds are too strong against drawing two cards when the game is played without a joker. When a joker is used, as in casino poker, it has any value the player wishes to give it. But we'll discuss this later.

In late position, we are in a good spot to steal a high ante, and with a pat hand headed by even a 9, we can raise an opener, but only one player. If another player has called the opener, we can still call, but if the other player has raised the opener, our 9-high pat hand isn't going to mean much. We can throw it away.

With a 7-high pat hand, we want to raise, no matter what position we're in. They're solid cards and any 7-high or lower hand is a favorite to win. Play aggressively with these cards. With an 8-high hand we can raise if we're in the last three positions; otherwise we call.

On drawing hands, it's very difficult to raise, because we have to draw to win, and raising on expectations is usually bad poker. However, with a large ante and late position, if we hold a really smooth four-card hand, such as 432A or 532A or even 5432, we can give it a shot and raise. If we draw solidly, we have the game won.

But we must take position into consideration. We don't

want to raise in an earlier position with those cards, because players behind us can reraise and then we must go all the way with these cards and put in a lot of money before we can even be sure of a winning hand.

And the higher the ante, the more aggressive we should become. In late position we want to steal that ante whenever we can, and so, even with an 8-high pat hand and late position, we can raise. But if there's a normal or small ante, there's no sense in trying to get the ante and risking a raise. We can wait it out past the draw.

After the draw, we again must be aware of our position at the table. When in a late position, we can gauge the relative strengths of the hands, and if two or more players are in without a raise and our hand is a 7-high we can raise them with impunity.

Don't worry about playing aggressively. The players you face won't all be strong; many will draw two cards time after time, a deadly giveaway of their weakness. Punish those weak players who play on expectations. Very rarely will they draw out on you, but in the meantime you'll be beating them out of hand after hand.

We spoke before of a "smooth" hand. Let's clarify this. In lowball poker parlance, hands can be either "smooth" or "rough." Let's examine an 8-high hand to see the difference.

A hand containing 87543 is a "rough" hand, because the next-highest card is a 7, whereas 8543A is a "smooth" hand, with the 5 being next-highest. At a showdown with 8-high hands, which occurs often, the smooth hand will win, of course. Play more aggressively with smooth hands; be careful about rough hands, especially rough 8- and 9-high hands.

Let's now summarize the strategy for lowball, draw poker.

1. Never draw more than one card, unless the game is played with a blind, and you're the blind and are forced to bet.

2. Be aware of the ante structure of the game. With a high ante, play more aggressively, attempting to steal the ante on the first round of betting. With a normal or low ante, play more conservatively.

3. Your position is important. It takes stronger cards to open in early position, or raise in early position, than it does in later position.

4. You can open with pat hands, but never with a hand headed by a jack, queen, or king. Only in seventh or eighth position can we open with a 10-high pat hand. In fourth, fifth, or sixth position we can open with a 9-high, and only an 8-high or better can open for us in the first three positions.

5. Drawing hands can also be opened, but only when holding a 7-high in the first four positions, an 8-high in the fifth and sixth positions, and a 9-high in the seventh position. In last position, we can open a 10-high drawing hand.

6. With a 9-high pat hand, we can raise in very late position, but only if there's one player in with us. With an 8-high hand we raise only in the last three positions with this pat holding. With a 7-high pat hand we raise from any position.

7. We can raise with a drawing hand if it's very smooth, such as one headed by a 5 or 4. These hands are best raised from a later position.

8. We should gauge the strength of the players at the table, and play more aggressively against those that are weak and stay in to draw cards. Against a player who constantly draws two cards, we should be super-aggressive.

9. With hands headed by an 8 or 9, the smoother the hand, the better for us. Be careful about playing a rough hand too aggressively.

10. Always be aware of position in the game, and if possible, change seats to be behind stronger players, so that you're not reraised when punishing the weaker players. If a strong player has checked, you can then deal directly with weaker players.

CALIFORNIA CLUB POKER, LOWBALL DRAW

In California clubs, this game is played with a joker as the fifty-third card. The joker is wild, and can be used to advantage by the player, for it can be made into any card he desires.

There's also a blind bettor in these games, who must open if he's to the left of the dealer. These two factors make the game different from the private game.

With a joker in your hand, you can play a more aggressive game, for two reasons. First, more hands can be formed by using the joker. Second, there's less chance of pairing a card when drawing one card to the hand. And of course, if you have the joker, no other player has it.

With the joker, you can raise and draw much more aggressively, and should do so. You can play four-card holdings with the joker headed by a 7 in second position, and with an 8 in positions 3 through 6. The earlier positions call for a smoother 8 than the later positions. The seventh position can be played with a rough 9 and the final position with a rough 10.

Study Chapter Eight, "California Poker Games," as well as the preceding sections of this chapter, before attempting to play in any of the California clubs.

SEVEN-CARD STUD, LOWBALL

This is the only stud game we're going to discuss in terms of lowball, because the five-card stud, low-ball, game is rarely played. In lowball, unlike the high version of five-card stud, one card can destroy a hand. That's why, in a five-card version, players will give no action to the game, and it's not a good money game.

For example, suppose Player A holds 5437, with the 5 in the hole, and Player B holds 10864 with the 10 in the hole.

This still doesn't mean too much, because if Player A draws a 3 on the last card and Player B draws a king, there's nothing Player A can do but fold. There's no opportunity to bluff.

In seven-card stud, lowball, however, three cards are concealed, and the player can choose his best low hand from seven cards. This makes for much more interesting play and infinitely more action.

The standard fifty-two-card deck is used, without jokers. The rank of the cards and the hands are as explained in the beginning of this chapter.

The pot can be won in the usual two ways, either by best hand at the showdown, or with only one player remaining in the game to claim the pot.

Antes

There is normally no ante in seven-card stud, lowball, which is also called "Razz." There will be an ante, however, in the casino games played in Nevada.

Betting Limits

The betting is two-tiered, with the lower bet one half the value of the higher bet, and the stakes can be $1–$2, $5–$10, $15–$30, and so forth. In Razz the general rule is that the lower limit is used until Fifth Street, then the higher limit takes over.

Betting Rounds

There are five betting rounds, with the opening round taking place on Third Street when each player in the game has three cards, two face down and one exposed.

The Deal

The deal moves around clockwise, with each player getting a chance to deal. There is no advantage to being dealer. The dealer deals one card to the player on his left, face down, and repeats this till all players have one card, then he gives each player another card face down, and a third face up, in the same manner.

After all players have three cards, two in the hole and one exposed, the first round of betting begins.

First Betting Round

Low card brings it in; that is, opens the betting. When two players have the same low card, the player closest to the dealer's left opens the betting. Once the bet is made, and it is mandatory for the low player to open on this round, all players in turn can call, raise, or fold, beginning with the player to the opener's left. There can be no checks on the first round of play.

After all bets have been made, the dealer takes up the stock of cards and deals another card face up to the players, and we begin the second round of betting.

Second and Subsequent Betting Rounds

The lowest hand showing on Fourth Street brings in the action. If two players have identical low hands, the player closest to the dealer's left opens. This player may check if he desires; he's still in the game if he decides not to put in an opening bet. Then each player in turn, beginning with the player to the low hand's left, can either check or open. When a player finally opens the betting, all players in turn after him who haven't checked can call, raise, or fold. Those players who have already checked can either call or fold; they can't raise.

On Fifth, Sixth, and Seventh streets, the betting is in the higher tier, and raises are in multiples of that limit. For example, if the game is a $5–$10 one, then bets from Fifth Street on would be $10, and raises would be in $10 increments.

After all bets are in on Seventh Street, if there are two or more players remaining in the game there's a showdown.

The Showdown

At the showdown, the player called shows his hand first. If his hand is the lowest, the other players can concede without showing theirs. To form the best hand, the player uses the lowest of his seven cards, if they are odd. For example, if a player held 39K510J3, his lowest hand would be J10953. He'd disregard the other 3 since it would pair the 3 he held in the hole, and five odd cards are stronger than any one-pair hand in low poker.

If a player is new at the game, he should show his cards rather than concede, because he may overlook a low hand. There are seven cards to choose from, and this is often a difficult game to comprehend for beginners, who forget that straights and flushes don't count. If in doubt, show your cards at the showdown and let them speak for themselves.

STRATEGIC PRINCIPLES OF SEVEN-CARD STUD, LOWBALL

There's one important fact to remember in this game. Unlike the high version of seven-card stud, in lowball the player is always holding drawing cards. In the high version, if you start off with three aces, for example, you probably will win the pot no matter what you draw.

But in Razz subsequent cards can destroy your hand.

For example, suppose you start off with A23, the best possible cards to hold on Third Street. This doesn't mean you're going to win if you start drawing bad cards. Although you're "perfect" in the hole, the term for a very smooth hand, your next few cards can be 3K2 and all you have is a headache, with two pairs and a king-high hand at best. You're dead at this point, and another hand that began 4Q7, then drew 610J, has you beat no matter what comes up on Seventh Street.

Never disregard this fact of life about Razz. It's a game that is always on the come till you are able to form a solid low hand, and you can't do this till Fifth Street.

The first and most important strategic consideration, as is usual with stud games, is what cards to stay in with on Third Street. The minimum holding should usually be a 7-high hand, and of course, the smoother the better. By smooth we mean a 732; a rough hand would be 764. But any holding headed by a 7 is worth playing. You can also play an 8-high hand if the other players' cards are pretty high. For example, you are dealt 856 and an open 4 brings it in, but the other cards showing are 9, jack, 10, queen, 6, and 5.

The 856 is a good hand to play here, a raise may even be in order, because the board cards are all terrible with the exception of the 4, 5 and 6, and the 5 and 6 are cards that would have hurt you if you drew them, so their exposure is in your favor.

So pay attention not only to your own hand, but also to the other players' cards on Third Street. And think in terms of smoothness. 92A can be a desirable opening hand, because of the 2 and ace; it would be an even better hand if the 9 was exposed.

But if the board is full of low cards, then only go in with a 7-high hand. Play conservatively, because draws will destroy a lot of your hands. You don't need bad hands to start with, with two strikes on you from the start.

If you make an 8-high hand by Fifth Street, you're a favorite over any drawing hand that isn't made yet, and can play aggressively, making the drawing hand pay for the privilege of trying to beat you.

On the other hand, if you hold a very smooth drawing hand on Fifth Street and figure the opponent has a very rough 9, such as 98, you can make a bet here, even bet into him, giving him the opportunity to raise you. But if the 9-high hand is smooth, then you're an underdog with your drawing hand on Fifth Street.

Keep in mind not only the cards on the board on Third Street, but also all small cards you see. If they're small cards that would pair your hand, keep playing, but if they're cards that you need, they're going to hurt you, and you should play cautiously or fold if enough small cards you need are showing.

For example, if you hold 754, and see a couple of 7s and 5s, that's fine for you. There's less likelihood of pairing with those cards. But if 3s, 2s, and aces are out on the board in abundance, they're cards taken away from your hand, and the chances of pairing or getting high cards on the draw is much stronger.

Let's now summarize the strategy for seven-card stud, lowball.

1. Never forget that this is a drawing game, in which your hand is on the come at all times until you make a five-card hand on Fifth, Sixth, or Seventh streets.

2. The best hand on Third Street is a 7-high (or lower high hand). An 8-high hand can also be played, if smooth, and a 9-high hand can be played if extremely smooth and if the board is full of high cards.

3. Examine the board carefully on Third Street to determine your strategy. With a weak or normal board, that is, cards showing, you can play aggressively and raise with all 7-high hands and even 8-high smooth hands.

4. If you have really low Third Street cards, such as 43A

or any 4-high hand, don't raise at the outset. Slow play this hand and don't give it away.

5. Any drawing hand on Fifth Street is an underdog to an 8-high formed hand, or a smooth 9-high formed hand. If you're an underdog, don't raise on the come. You can play for the draw and hope to hit perfectly, but wait till you have the hand before raising an already formed 8- or 9-high smooth hand.

6. Examine the board constantly and see how the cards showing, especially the small ones, are affecting your hand. When cards that could pair your cards are on the board, it makes your hand stronger. When small cards you need are on the board, that weakens your hand.

7. When you make a hand by Fifth Street, you're a favorite over any drawing hand, if it's headed by an 8 or smooth 9. Make the opponent pay to see you; be aggressive and raise if you can.

8. Keep in mind that Razz attracts weak players, for experts consider it the least skillful of poker games. That's because draws can destroy hands, and thus the luck of the draw is very important. Therefore, gauge your opposition, and go after the weak players with aggressive play.

9. Weak players in Razz will generally start with hands you wouldn't play and continue to play higher hands that you'd fold. They are praying to get a perfect draw. Punish them.

NEVADA CASINO POKER—RAZZ

Razz is played in a number of clubs in Las Vegas, and a game can usually be found. These games aren't the first choice of top players, because of the luck factor. Even starting with solid cards is no guarantee that you're going to make a hand that can win.

In the casinos, the main difference between Razz and

the private game is who brings it in. In the casinos, high card must bring it in on Third Street, and this makes for more action in the game.

Otherwise the same strategy prevails as we've already discussed. There might be more raising on the opening round because the opener has the worst card showing, and if you're in a late position with decent cards you can try to steal the ante and the pot by a raise.

Otherwise, play according to our strategic principles. But keep in mind the luck factor, which makes Razz an aggravating game to play. You can start with the best hand and watch a mediocre player draw out and beat you.

VI

HIGH-LOW POKER

High-low poker is usually played as a seven-card stud game, both privately and in casinos. That's the perfect type of game for high-low, because, with three concealed cards and seven cards from which to form one's best hand, the action is nonstop, and it becomes a terrific game.

At one time, five-card draw and stud were played frequently as a high-low game, but both these games have simply petered out, and it's hard to find any game of five-card high-low. That's why we're going to concentrate on the seven-card stud high-low game.

There are basically two variations of the game, the "declare" game, which is played privately, and the "split" game, which is the variation played most often in casinos.

Each will be discussed in full, for when you understand the concepts and know how to play well, you can make a lot of money in each variation.

The basic concept of high-low poker is that no one kind of hand is played for. High hands and low hands have an equal chance in this game. If one player has a high hand and another a low one, the pot will be split between them if one declares high and the other low. The third option makes this game even more exciting: A player can go for high-low and win the entire pot.

For example, let's assume that in a hand of seven-card stud, high-low, there are three players remaining at the showdown. This is a declare game, so all players must declare their hands at the same time. This is easily done with chips. A white chip held in a fist means low, a red chip high, and a white and a red chip means high-low. There are other ways of declaring hands, with coins, for example, but this is one very simple way.

Player A declares low, Player B declares high, and Player C declares high-low. These are the hands:

Player A holds 85432

Player B holds KKJJ9

Player C holds 76543

Player C would win the entire pot. His low hand is better than Player A's, because it is a 7-high compared to A's 8-high (straights and flushes don't count when declaring low, only in determining high hands), and Player C's straight is better than Player B's two pairs.

When a player declares high-low, he must have both the best low and the best high hand at the showdown, otherwise he forfeits the entire pot, and is no longer in contention.

Suppose we had this situation. Player A and Player B both declare high, and Player C declares high-low. These are their hands:

Player A holds QQQ43

Player B holds AA6610

Player C holds 999J2 and J9432

Player C forms two hands but the low hand doesn't matter since no one else declared low. For him to win the pot, he has to win both high and low. But since Player A's high is better than his, he loses the entire pot. If player C had declared low, he would have won half the pot by default, *no matter what he held*.

If only one player at the showdown declares one way, and the others declare the other way, the first player gets half the pot automatically, since no one else declared the same way he did.

SEVEN-CARD STUD, HIGH-LOW, DECLARE

We've already explained the declare concept of this game. Declaring is done at the showdown, and all players declare simultaneously, not in order. The coins or chips are placed in each player's fist, then all shown at once. Then the cards are shown.

The standard fifty-two-card deck is used, without jokers. The rank of the cards and the hands are as explained in Chapter One, for high hands, and Chapter Five, for low hands.

The pot can be won in various ways. If a player declares high-low and his hand is best both high and low, he wins the entire pot. If no one declares high-low, and several players declare high but only one player declares low, the low declarer wins half the pot and the best high hand wins the other half of the pot.

If all players declare only one way, for example, high, then the best high hand wins the entire pot. If only one player remains in the game at the showdown (an extremely rare situation) he can claim the entire pot.

Number of Players

This game is best played with between six and eight players, but even a smaller game, because of the nature of high-low, can be a high-action event.

Antes

There is normally no ante in this game, except in the casino version known as "high-low split."

Betting Limits

The betting is two-tiered, with the larger bet double the smaller bet, and no bets are permitted between these two limits. The higher bet is used when a pair is showing, or on Sixth and Seventh streets.

Betting Rounds

There are five betting rounds, with the opening round taking place on Third Street, when each player has his initial three cards, two hidden and one face up.

The Deal

The deal moves clockwise around the table, with each player getting the deal in order. There is no advantage to being dealer. The cards are first shuffled and then given to the player on the dealer's right to be cut. After the cut they're restacked.

Starting with the player to the dealer's left, each player gets one card face down, then, after all the players have this card, another is dealt face down and a third face up to each player in the same order.

After all the players have three cards, two in the hole and one exposed, the first round of betting begins.

First Betting Round

The high card brings it in. If two or more players have the same high card, the player closest to the dealer's left opens the betting, at the lower limit. Thus, in a $5–$10 game, the opening bet will be $5.

The high card can't check on this round of betting, he must bet. After he opens, then each player in turn can call, raise, or fold. There is usually a lot of raising done, on all rounds of play, because players are going for high or low hands, or both, and a player with drawing expectations can be in a good position to raise. For example, if the pot is opened by a king, a player holding 543 of different suits may raise, for his hand can go both ways, high and low. Another player with a low three-flush, such as 75A, may reraise, again holding a hand that goes both ways, for he may feel that he can "scoop" the pot, that is, win both ways.

After all bets are in, the dealer takes up the stock of cards and deals another card face up to the players, and we begin the second round of betting.

Second and Subsequent Betting Rounds

On Fourth Street, which is the second betting round, the high hand opens the betting. On this and all the following betting rounds, the high hand has the option of checking or betting. If the high hand checks, he isn't out of play. He has the opportunity to call a bet (though he may not raise) when it is his turn again. If the high hand checks, the player to his left can bet or check, and each player in turn, if no one before him has opened, has this option. After a player opens, all players behind him, who haven't yet checked, can call, raise, or fold. Those players who have already checked can only call a bet, not raise, or of course, they may fold.

If there's an open pair, the bets will be at the higher limit. However, on Sixth Street or Seventh Street, even if no pair is showing, the bets are at the higher limit.

If more than one player remains at the end of the betting on Seventh Street, there's a showdown. At this point, each remaining player has seven cards, four open and three closed. The final card dealt on Seventh Street is dealt face down.

The Showdown

The showdown is unlike those in ordinary seven-card stud, either high or lowball, because here the players must declare their intention to go high, low, or high-low.

This is done by placing an appropriate chip or chips in one's fist, unseen by all the other players and exposed only when all the other players remaining in the game expose theirs. We've mentioned one way of doing this (a white chip for low, red for high, white and red for high-low). Another would be to show a white chip for low, blue for high, and red for high-low. Or coins can be used, a penny for low, a dime for high, and a quarter for high-low. This method or any method used should be agreed upon before the game starts, and each player should have the correct coins or chips available for declaring.

After the fists are open, the players expose their cards. However, if one player declared low and the others high, the low player need not expose his cards, but can immediately take half the pot.

If some players declare high and others low, the best high hand wins half the pot, and the best low hand wins the other half. Low hands are ranked from 5432A upward, with this wheel being the best hand for low. Remember, in declaring for low, a player doesn't count flushes or straights.

Because seven cards are involved, a player can have a good low and a good high hand among these cards. He therefore can declare high-low if he feels he can win the whole pot, but if his cards are good enough to win only high or low, and not both, he forfeits his chance to claim any of the pot. He is out of the game, and the player with the best high hand takes high and the best low hand takes low and they split the pot.

STRATEGIC PRINCIPLES OF SEVEN-CARD STUD, HIGH-LOW, DECLARE

The ideal hand to hold from the outset is one that can scoop the pot, that is, take both ends, high and low. Therefore the hand will be one that is on the low side, but with possibilities of flushes and straights to bolster it.

A player holding a low three-straight such as 654, or a low flush possibility such as 64A in clubs is in a good spot here. High hands aren't as strong in declare, because you'll be going for one half the pot at best, and will have to beat other high hands, but a low hand can become a high hand as well, especially a drawing hand that can develop into a flush or straight.

The other ideal hand is one that is well camouflaged—for example, if you're holding what seems to be a low hand on the board, but is in reality a high hand, or vice versa. With these types of hands, you will get action from players on the other side. For instance, if the opponent thinks you and another player have low hands, while he has a high hand, he'll be raising at every opportunity, figuring that he'll get half of a pot both of you have to contribute to. In this situation, you can really trap the other player and create a monster pot for yourself.

Let's suppose that you're holding the following hand on Third Street—KK2 with the kings concealed. Your hand is well hidden. When you bet with the deuce showing, it could be a low or high hand, probably a low one. Your next card is a 7. Against you are two players on Fourth Street. One holds 86 and the other holds J9.

Obviously the J9 is going for a high hand. If he's trying for a low hand, he's third-best on the board, and doomed. The 86 is in there probably going for low hand, maybe even for a straight. But we have to figure him for low, which the holder of the J9 also figures.

On Fifth Street the J9 bets. What do you do? Here a

raise is in order. Your 72 is lower than the 86 and by raising, you appear to be trying to drive out the 86 and split the pot with the high J9. But the 86, a weak player, calls, and the J9 reraises. Why not? He figures that both of you are fighting for low and he'll be grabbing one half of the pot. You call and the 86 calls. On the next draw you buy a 2, pairing your 2s on board. The J9 gets a 9 and the 86 gets a jack.

The 9s are high, and bet. You raise again, and now the 86J hesitates. His jack hurt but your pair of 2s gives him hope for low, so he calls. The 9s reraise, and you reraise him, and now the 86J is in real trouble. He decides to call; the 9s reraise, and you reraise. Again the 86J calls, as does the J99.

On Sixth Street, following each player's buy, the hands look like this:

You: KK2724
A: **86J10
B: **J995

The 9s bet, and you raise. The 86 didn't like the looks of your 4. With a 742 on board, and two little babies (small cards) in the hole, you would have him beat all around, so he finally folds. Now, you're just where you want to be, head to head with the jacks. He calls your raise, figuring that he has half the pot, and there's no sense in betting anymore.

On Seventh Street, he checks, which shows that he's still satisfied. You buy an odd card, and can now check and call high and stun the jacks hand. It turns out he had jacks up, and you win the entire pot.

You've built up the pot beautifully, and what's more, you had a perfect escape if your opponent had improved on Sixth Street and his board showed, for instance, J99J. All you do is call low and you've got half the pot.

Which brings us to the next strategic principle. If possible, go with a hand that can scoop, but if you have either a low or a high hand, make certain it's the best, otherwise you might get caught in the middle the way the holder of the 86J10 was. If you're low with another player and the third player is high, you'll be raised to kingdom come by the third player, and if you can't even take the low, you'll be buried in this situation. Even if it's a borderline situation where you're holding 865 against the opponent's 876 on board, and you can't figure if he's perfect in the hole and smoother with his 8 than you, get out. You can't afford to be trapped.

On the other hand, always trap the other players when you can. The best way is with a concealed hand that looks the opposite of what it is. The second-best way is to play a low hand that can develop high as well while the others are playing high hands. You must raise here and play as aggressively as possible. Build up the pot for yourself in this game. Seven-card high-low, declare, is a perfect game for this. A lot of weak players are attracted to this game because they think it's one of luck, that they're bound to buy something either high or low. But it's not that type of game at all.

As we've seen, psychology plays a big part in this game. You must disguise your hand and your intentions, or give the wrong signals, which is even better strategy. In the example we showed before the jacks-over-9s holder never guessed that you would call high.

If you avoid the trap situations, where you're fighting for one half the pot with another player while the odd player is raising both of you, you'll be way ahead of the game. The way to avoid these traps is not to play for one side, especially the high side, unless you have disguised cards. Go for the low side, with an out of getting high cards out of the hand, such as a low hand turning into a flush.

And remember about the escape. We showed how, by eliminating the weak player and playing one-to-one against a player whose intentions you know, you can always declare the opposite way if he improves his hand, especially if he's clearly going for high.

Let's now summarize the strategies involved in seven-card stud, high-low, declare.

1. The ideal hand to hold is one that can scoop the pot, that is, take both sides, high and low. This will always be a low hand, with flush and straight and sometimes trip possibilities.

2. Another ideal hand is one that is disguised, so that other players, from looking at your board, will think you are playing for the opposite of what you really are going for.

3. Therefore, when holding a disguised hand, such as a high pair in the hole with a "baby" (a small card) on the board, play aggressively to give the impression that you're going the other way.

4. You must create monster pots for yourself in this game, and the best way to do this is to raise when alone for one side while others are battling for the other side.

5. Another good position is to hold a scoop hand that could possibly take both sides, with one assured. Raise all you can.

6. When disguising your hand, raise the player who seems to have the opposite side while you're supposedly battling it out with a weaker player on your side. For example, if your board looks low but you're going for high and are in against one player who is going for low and another who thinks high is all his, raise the high player, trapping the "other" low player and forcing him out.

7. Don't get caught in the middle yourself. If you are uncertain if you have best low, and there's a player alone with a high hand raising, get out. These situations drain your bankroll at the poker table.

8. Always try to have an escape when head-to-head or in with two other players. If they keep drawing strongly one way, even against your type of hand, declare the other way, and reserve half the pot for yourself.

9. This is a game full of psychology. Learn the strengths and weaknesses of your opponents while at the table. Punish the weak players, who are often in this kind of game, thinking it's pure luck.

10. Don't be afraid to play aggressively. You must do this, not only to take control, but also to disguise your hand at times, and to send out the wrong signals, especially if you have a disguised holding or are in a solid position to scoop the pot.

HIGH-LOW SPLIT—NEVADA CASINO GAME

The basic difference between the private declare game and high-low split is that, in the casino game, *the cards speak for themselves*. At the showdown, there is no declaration of high, low, or high-low. Instead, the players put out their cards and if one player has the best high and the best low he wins the entire pot. If one player has the best low and another the best high hand, the pot is split.

This eliminates a great deal of psychological play. It's still good to disguise your hand, but only for betting, not for declaration purposes.

When playing the casino game, it's important to play hands that can "scoop" the pot, that is, take both high and low. With this in mind, the best kind of hands to play are low hands that can develop into a straight or flush.

In order to play low hands correctly, it's a good idea to throw away hands that don't draw well on Fourth Street. For example, if you have a 765 at the outset and draw a face card, a jack, queen, or king, it's now a tough hand to play. When going for low, unless you draw good cards, your hand can be destroyed quickly by bad cards, pairing cards, or face cards.

This is essential strategy for high-low split. There's no way to outfox the players at the showdown; you must try for both sides of the pot, and have at least one side solid, so as to escape with half the pot.

In the casino game, there's always an ante, which may be low, normal, or high, depending on the casino or the game. On the opening round of play, Third Street, the high card brings it in. However, after this round of betting, the low hand acts first. This is another difference between the casino and the private games.

Study the preceding sections of this chapter, and alter your strategy to accommodate the casino game by playing more low hands. If you want to seriously play high-low split, start in a small casino game. Only if you can win at low stakes should you play for higher stakes.

VII

TEXAS HOLD 'EM

This game, also known simply as Hold 'Em, is popular in the Nevada casinos and is among the most complex of poker games.

Each player gets two cards face down, and then five cards are put on the board, face up, which are used with the two cards to form the best five-card hand. The five face-up cards are dealt three at a time, then one card, then the last. Altogether there are four betting rounds. All casino games have an ante.

The standard fifty-two-card deck is used, without jokers, and the rank of the hands and cards is the same as in high poker. The number of players can run to fifteen; usually eight to eleven are playing.

The Deal

The house dealer shuffles and cuts the cards, and burns one—that is, pulls the first card off the top of the deck and removes it from play. He burns a card on each additional round of play.

There is a button moved around the table to each player in turn, signifying an imaginary dealer. Position is important in Hold 'Em.

Each player receives two cards face down, one at a time. When each player has two cards, the first round of betting commences.

First Betting Round

Usually there is a blind, the first player to the button's left. He makes a bet, and each player in turn must call the bet, raise, or fold. After all bets are in, the dealer burns another card.

The Flop

Three cards are now laid out on the table. These are face up and are community cards, which may be used by any player in the game to form his own hand.

Second Betting Round

After the flop, the betting commences again with the player to the button's left, or, if he's out of play, the player closest to the button. This second betting round is still at the lower limit of betting. In a $10–$20 game, all bets are $10 and raises are in units of $10.

Fourth Street

Four cards will now be on board, with the dealer putting out a single card to add to the flop. The betting continues in the same manner as on the second betting round. After all bets are in, the last card is dealt. On Fourth Street, all bets are at the highest limit; in a $10–$20 game, they're at $20.

Fifth Street

A fifth card is now dealt face up. Five cards will now be on board, which each player remaining in the game combines with his two hole cards to form his hand. After betting on Fifth Street, if more than one player remains in the game there is a showdown.

The Showdown

The player called shows his cards. Then if any player in turn feels he can beat that hand, he shows his cards. A player may concede without showing his or her cards. The best hand at the showdown wins the pot.

STRATEGIC CONSIDERATIONS

The most important strategic question is what cards to stay in with before the flop. Remember, you only have two cards, and will not get any more hole cards, while you'll be sharing the board with the other players.

The best cards are the following: a pair of aces; a pair of kings; ace and king suited (same suit); a pair of queens; ace and king offsuited; ace and queen or king and queen of the same suit.

Then pairs from 8s to jacks can be played, and finally ace and jack, king and jack, queen and jack, and jack and 10 of the same suit.

These are the strongest cards you can hold in descending order. Position also counts. You can divide positions as follows: the blind and the second through fourth seats, early position; fifth to seventh, middle position; eighth to eleventh, late position. Unlike other stud games, in which position depends on the cards showing on the board, in Hold 'Em position never changes; it's fixed by the deal.

Don't stay in with marginal hands in bad position, because you'll be contributing to the pot time after time. It's best to go in with the strongest hands and play them aggressively; raise with them before the flop. This way you take control and get rid of players who might draw out against you.

In late position you can play much looser than in early position, but it depends on how many players are already in the game at this point. The lower marginal hands and even a low-ranked pair or low connected cards, such as 78 of one suit, take on value here. But against a raise or two, they might be thrown away before the flop. Unraised situations call for them to be played in late position.

When you have the top hand, such as aces, you want to play aggressively. Don't be a caller, be a raiser. Those going for flushes and straights will have to pay to stay in; don't give them free rides or easy betting situations.

If you are dealt a drawing hand, and the flop is in your favor, again play aggressively and raise. For example, suppose you were dealt the king and queen of diamonds as your hole cards. The flop comes up 9(H), 6(D), 3(D). This flop is very favorable for you. You now have a four-flush and no card on the flop will give any other player a higher pair than your king. If an ace showed on this flop, you'd have to worry about beating a pair of aces.

Play the best cards, play position, and gauge your opposition. You'll find Hold 'Em can be a lucrative money game. When you have the goods, make those weaker players who are in there hoping to draw lucky pay for the privilege of doing so.

In the casinos, get into the smaller games first. Only if you can win money in these games should you graduate to the bigger stake games. If you're losing, don't blame luck. Restudy the game, improve your play, and then try again. Only play in bigger stake games when you're a consistent winner at the smaller games.

VIII

CALIFORNIA POKER GAMES

California has passed statutes allowing draw poker to be played legally in selected areas throughout the state, but only draw poker is legal. There are no legal stud games permitted. The two versions of draw, high and low, are played in close to five hundred licensed card clubs up and down the state of California, but the center of activity is in a suburb of Los Angeles called Gardena.

Gardena bills itself as the "draw-poker capital of the world," and it might very well be that. In the Nevada casinos, where poker is also permitted, the clubs have poker games mainly as a sideline to produce more income from gamblers. Many of the Nevada poker rooms within larger casinos are rented to operators who run the game, but in Gardena, that's all you'll find in the way of gambling—draw poker.

Club Rules

In the California clubs, there are strict rules concerning the way the games are to be played, and how the patrons are to conduct themselves during play. These rules are printed in booklets and are available in the clubs for all the patrons. It's very important that a player read over the rules before playing, because if he disregards some or even one of them, he may find himself forfeiting not only a bet, but also the entire pot.

Several of the rules are for the benefit of the patrons, and make good common sense. No drinking is allowed during the games, and there are no bars in any of the clubs. An intoxicated player will not be permitted to play in the games.

Unlike the Nevada games, where there is a dealer working for the house, who rakes off money from every pot for the casino's benefit and deals all the games, in California there is no rake at all, just an hourly rental. And there is no house dealer.

The patrons play among themselves, and deal the cards in turn. Each hour their rent is due and it is dependent upon the size of the stakes in any particular game. The bigger the game, the more each player must pay by the hour.

The games are orderly and the atmosphere is fairly sedate for a gambling club situation. There are security guards in evidence, and floormen to assist with difficult situations or to settle disputes among players.

Although no alcohol will be served, the clubs generally serve food at reasonable prices, and also have television and sitting rooms available for the patrons to relax in.

In the larger clubs of Gardena, there are various limit games available, both in high poker and in lowball, and a patron wishing to play in any particular game at a certain limit gives his name to a boardman who puts down only the player's initials on a blackboard in chalk. When there's an opening in that type of game, the player's initials will be called, and he'll be directed to the correct table.

Cards

All of the draw games use the standard fifty-two-card deck with one joker added to it. Thus, the players will be playing with a fifty-three-card deck throughout. This joker is called a "bug" by patrons of the game.

In high games, the joker is a limited wild card, used only as an ace or to form flushes or straights. Otherwise it has no value.

In high draw, as played in California clubs, the best possible hand is five aces, with the joker counting as one ace.

In lowball, the joker is a true wild card and can be made into any card the player desires to improve his hand.

The Games

High draw and lowball draw are the basic games one will encounter in the clubs. In high draw the game is usually jacks or better, except for an open blind game, which is also known as California draw. In this game, there are several variations possible. The player to the left of the dealer must open blind, but it's a live blind, so that he can come back and raise when it's his turn again.

This is the usual variation, which means that there are no requirements for opening, such as jacks or better. In the second variation, the next player must also bet blind, but must raise. And the third variation has the third player reraising the second.

In the third variation, there's an awful lot of money on the table before the fourth player decides to act on his hand. It's a high-action game.

All the lowball games have a blind bettor, who is a live blind.

There are various limit games, always with two tiers, with the higher limit double the lower limit, and within the game of high poker, the betting range can increase if betting is not opened by any player in jacks or better. A $5 draw game, which initially is $5–$10, can become $10–$20 if no one can open and the cards have to be dealt again.

The $10 draw in high poker also increases in certain games up to a $20–$40 game. Be careful about choosing the game you're going to play and be sure you understand the rules and betting and ante structure of each game; otherwise you might find yourself way over your head.

Players

The table limit is eight players. That's a full game in any variation. At least three players must be sitting at a table for the game to begin.

Rank of Hands—High Draw

These are the relative rankings, with best hand first:

1. Five aces (four aces and the joker)
2. Royal flush
3. Straight flush
4. Four of a kind
5. Full house
6. Flush
7. Straight
8. Three of a kind
9. Two pair
10. One pair

Rank of Hands—Low Draw

The very best hand is 5432A, known as a wheel or bicycle, with the joker wild. This is a better hand than the natural 5432A without the joker. Then comes 6432A, and so forth. See Chapter Five for further ranking of hands, if in doubt.

Rental Fees

The following are representative rental fees at the California clubs:

Game	Fee
$1–$2	$1
$2–$4	$1.25
$3–$6	$1.50
$5 –$10	$2
$10–$20	$3

Antes

All games require an ante. They are generally below normal in high draw, with an ante of 25¢ for $1–$2, $2–$4, and $3–$6 games, 50¢ for the $5–$10 games, and $1 for the $10–$20 games.

In lowball, the ante is a normal one, with 10% of the high bet the usual ante.

Buy-Ins

A "buy-in" is the amount of money a player must convert into chips to start a game with. In the California clubs, it's generally ten times the minimum bet. Thus, in a $5–$10 game, the buy-in is $50. Chips of standard denominations, from 25¢ to $20, are provided by the individual clubs, and the games are played with these chips rather than with cash.

The Deal

The deal moves around the table in the usual clockwise manner. No player may pass up the deal. After the dealer shuffles the cards, the player to his right cuts them. If any player at the table believes that the cards haven't been shuffled properly, he may demand that the cards be mixed again.

The cards are dealt in the usual manner, beginning with the player to the dealer's left, one at a time, face down, until each player at the table has five cards. Then the stock of cards is put to one side by the dealer, who puts a chip on the deck, capping it, so that it can't be handled.

There's a betting round before the draw, and another after the draw. Before dealing more cards to the players, the dealer must "burn" the top card, that is, put it to one side out of play before giving the players their draw cards.

Special California Club Rules for High Draw

1. Jacks or better are required to open the betting.
2. The opening bettor must show his openers in order to win the pot.
3. When splitting his openers (discarding one of the cards that allowed him to open), the player must declare that he is doing so and protect the split card by turning it face up under a chip.
4. The game is check and raise.
5. Before the draw, if a card is dealt exposed by the dealer, the player must take it. After the draw, an exposed card can't be taken.

Rules for Low Draw

1. If a player passes before the draw, the player is out of the game.
2. There is no check and raise after the draw.
3. Before the draw, any exposed card of 7 or under must be taken by the player. After the draw, no exposed cards can be taken.
4. If a 7-high or better hand has been checked, the

player checking it can't win an additional bet. If a 7-high hand is checked, provided it's the best 7-high hand (lowest), all other action is void.

House Rules—California Clubs

1. Players can't ante for other players.
2. Husband and wife, father and son, or close relatives can't play at the same table.
3. Any player can draw five cards.
4. A player who drops a card on the floor must still play that card.
5. Cards exposed face up in the deck are dead and can't be used.
6. On the draw, when a dealer exposes a player's card, it's a dead card, and the player shall receive another card after all the other players have received their cards.
7. If the dealer deals a card off the table, it's dead, unless it's the dealer's card.

PLAYING STRATEGY IN THE CALIFORNIA CLUBS

Before playing in any of these clubs, make sure you know correct strategy as outlined in the sections of this book on draw poker, jacks or better (see Chapter Three), and draw poker, lowball (see Chapter Five).

There are many tight players and a number of professional players in these games. Many have played for years. You don't want to enter a club with a vague notion of how the game is played. Make sure you know what you're doing, or your money will vanish pretty quickly.

You must play tight. There's very little bluffing in these games, and the players are there hoping to trap a newcomer or amateur. For example, in the high draw game, where jacks or better open, a number of players will check even three-of-a-kind hands before the draw, and then hit you with a raise.

You'll be among strangers. Cheating can occur, or collusion, with players acting as partners and splitting their winnings away from the club. Be suspicious and alert in these games. They're run as honestly as possible, but still, there are always cheats and sharps looking for the unwary.

It's extremely important that you gauge the strength of the players at the table. You should know what good play is; and when you see players disregarding the rules for strong play, you can put them down as weak opponents. For example, in high draw, a player under the gun who opens with jacks or queens is weak.

Unlike the private games, California clubs have the joker. It has limited value in high draw, but in lowball it's a powerful card indeed. When you hold the joker in lowball, you can easily make hands on the draw, because if you hold 653Joker, there are only three cards you can pair. If you buy a 7, you have a 7653A hand, and if you buy a 2, you have a super 6532A hand. When you hold the joker, you must play aggressively.

We suggest starting in low-limit games, till you get to know all the quirky rules of the clubs. If you can win in these games, move on to bigger games. If you can't win, don't blame luck or the cards. Restudy the strategy. Only when you win in low-limit games should you play higher-limit ones. And remember, the higher the limit, the stronger the competition. There are a number of players in these clubs who make a living there. Be careful and play well.

IX

NEVADA CASINO POKER

This chapter will deal with the essentials of casino poker. Each game played in the Nevada casinos has been covered in earlier chapters in a separate section at the end of the discussion of that particular game (such as seven-card stud, high).

Cards

The standard fifty-two-card deck is used for practically all games, without a joker. The games are played with smaller plastic cards that can take a beating.

Dealer

All cards are dealt by a house employee, not by the individual players. The dealer shuffles the cards and cuts them himself, makes sure the antes and bets are correct, and calls the game, telling which hand bets first, and announcing the status of play on any particular round.

The dealer also removes the house rake from each pot.

House Rake

There is no standard rental fee per hour in the Nevada casinos (except for certain big games). The dealer takes out money or chips from each pot during the course of play, and this is the house's cut for running the game, known as the "rake."

The rake may run from below 5% all the way to 25% in the smaller games. Some card rooms will limit the amount removed from a pot without regard to percentage, such as no more than $2.50 per pot from a $5–$10 game, no matter how much money is in the center of the table.

Don't play in any game where the rake exceeds 5%. Otherwise, the house will be your partner and you'll end up winning pots but not making money. A good rule is to avoid the smaller games, under $5–$10, where the rake is usually exorbitant.

Before sitting down, inquire about the house cut. Most of the time, there will be signs in the card room explaining the rake on any particular game.

Buy-Ins

The games are played mostly with chips, though cash can be used, but this will be converted into chips by the dealer unless the player says otherwise. For example, the player may make a final round bet with a $20 bill and if the bet is for $20, it will remain as cash. If the bill is more than the bet, it will immediately be converted into chips and the balance in chips given back to the player.

The games will often use standard casino chips, ranging in size from $1 to $100. In some small games there may be 25¢ chips, but most of the bigger casinos permit coins to be used, such as quarters and half dollars.

A buy-in is required. A buy-in is a minimum amount of chips the player must purchase and convert his cash to before entering the game. Ordinarily this is minimal, such as $100 for a $5–$10 game.

No matter what the buy-in calls for, we suggest that the player bring at least forty times the minimum bet to the table. This means $200 for a $5–$10 game. The money should be on the table. You may convert $100 into chips and leave the other $100 on the table, because the games in the casinos are played as "table stakes." This means that, for any particular pot, you cannot bet more than you have on the table in front of you. You aren't permitted to reach into your pocket to get more cash *during the play of a hand*.

But you are allowed to replenish your table stakes. If you start with $200 and get down to $75, for example, with some tough luck, bring out more money and put it on the table between deals or when you're not involved in the pot.

Don't ever be caught short: You don't want to have a winning hand and be forced to make a $5 bet, when your bet should be $20, because you neglected to put out money. Or worse, suppose you are caught short and can't even bet for several rounds of play because you ran out of table money?

Antes

Although there are exceptions, the ante structure is either normal or low, generally not high. Thus, in a stud poker game of $5–$10 the ante will usually be 50¢. The draw poker games will have a higher ante structure because of the nature of the game, and because there are only two betting rounds. This encourages action.

Expect to play with an ante, no matter what game you are entered in. This is a fairly constant rule in Nevada casinos.

Betting Limits

The usual rule is two-tiered, with the higher limit double the lower one, such as $5–$10 and so forth. However, in the smaller games, there may be more of a spread, such as $1–$3 and $1–$4. These games attract the tourists and amateurs, and aren't recommended. First of all, the rake is usually high and the action slow, and it's generally a waste of time to play, for you'll be giving money to the house rather than to the pot you win.

The higher the game, the better the players it will attract. Once you get to $10–$20 there will be several pros in the game, players who make a living at the game. Therefore, in the bigger games, you must play your best and keep your concentration. The best game to start with is the $5–$10 game. In the Vegas casinos, that's not really a big game; there's always less action in the casinos than there is in private games.

Check and Raise

In the stud and Hold 'Em games, expect to play check and raise. Some of the draw games are also check and raise, but it's not usual. If in doubt about the rules, ask the dealer, who will help you out with any questions you might have.

Even though the games are check and raise, the technique is not used that often, but it can be a potent weapon in the late rounds of play at stud.

In the lowball draw games, an early check may require a player to draw two cards if he later raises. Again, check the rules with the dealer, if in doubt.

Raises

As a general rule, only three raises are permitted on any particular round. This prevents a player from being trapped, and also holds down collusion between two players who might be secretly playing as partners.

Some casinos allow more raises per round, but the usual rule is that if only two players are left in the game, they can raise each other as often as they like. The risk of collusion has left the game.

The Button

In private games, the deal goes around the table in turn, but there's only one dealer in the casino games. To prevent any player from having a disadvantage as a result of position at the table in draw or Hold 'Em games, a button is moved around the table clockwise. This signifies the imaginary dealer, and the player to the left of the button bets and acts last.

When low or high card opens in a stud game, and two players hold identical opening cards, the opener is determined by suit. Clubs are the lowest, followed by diamonds, hearts, and spades. Thus if low card opens, and one player holds the deuce of clubs and another the deuce of diamonds, the club 2 is considered the lowest and must open.

Opening

This is called "bringing it in." To promote action, in high stud games, low card opens, and in low stud games, the high card is forced to open on the opening round of play.

The usual opening bet is less than the limit. For example, in a seven-card stud, high, game, if the betting limits are $5–$10, the opener on Third Street must open with $1 minimum. Since low card opens, the rule helps the opener, who saves $4 if he goes out right after a raise.

A final word: Be careful in the casino games. Don't drink, even though liquor is available, and don't play when tired or anxious. Keep alert. Don't play with money you can't afford to lose.

GLOSSARY OF POKER TERMS

Ace-high: Any hand or holding headed by an ace, such as a flush or straight.

Ante: Money or chips put into the pot before the deal to force action on the opening round. Also called Sweeten the pot.

Back in: Checking a strong hand, then raising after another player opens the betting in a check-and-raise game.

Bet: The money or chips put into the pot by a player.

Bicycle: The lowest possible holding, and thus the best hand in lowball poker; 5432A. Also called a wheel.

Blind opener: A player who must make a mandatory opening round bet, regardless of his hand's value.

Bluffing: Betting heavily on an inferior hand in order to drive the other players out of the game.

Board: The cards seen by the other players, either a player's hand or community cards.

Bring it in: See *Open*.

Burn a card: The removal of the top card from the stock by a dealer before cards are dealt.

Button: A small disc used where there's a permanent dealer to signify which player will bet and act first.

Buy: The drawing of a card by a player, either in stud or in draw poker.

Buy-In: The amount of money a player will change into chips before a game of poker.

Call, call a bet: Making a bet equal to the previous bet.

Check: Passing one's turn to bet. Also called pass.

Check and raise: A game in which a player may raise after first checking his hand.

Community cards: Cards that can be used by all players to form their best hand.

Cut, cut the cards: Dividing the deck into approximately two equal parts after the cards are shuffled and placing the former top half on the bottom of the deck.

Deuce: The poker slang term for the 2.

Discard pile: Cards put to one side, out of play, during a game of poker.

Draw: Additional cards dealt to a player during a game of stud, or cards exchanged for unwanted cards during draw poker.

Draw poker: A variation of poker in which all cards are dealt closed and a draw takes place after the first betting round.

Face card: A jack, queen, or king.

False openers: In jacks or better, the opening of the betting with cards inferior to a pair of jacks.

Fifth Street: The final round of betting in Hold 'Em; the third round of betting in seven-card stud.

Flop: The first three cards constituting the board in Hold 'Em.

Flush: A hand consisting of five cards of the same suit.

Fold: The act of dropping out of the game by discarding one's cards.

Four-flush: Four cards of the same suit.

Four of a kind: Four cards of any one rank, such as four jacks.

Fourth Street: The second round of betting in seven-card stud, and the next-to-last round of betting in Hold 'Em.

Free ride: A round of play in which no bets are made.

Full house: A hand that consists of three of a kind plus a pair.

Hand: Five cards that determine the player's best holding.

High, high poker: Any game or round in which the highest-ranked card or hand has precedence.

High hand: The best hand in any round of high poker.

High poker: That form of poker in which the high hand wins.

Hole card: The card or cards held by a player in stud poker unseen by the other players.

Inside straight: A holding of a four-straight in which an interior card is missing, such as 98–65.

Jacks or better, jackpots: A variation of draw poker in which a pair of jacks or higher holding is necessary to open the betting on the first round.

Joker: A fifty-third card of no particular rank or suit, which is often used as a wild card in the California clubs.

Kicker: A high-ranking odd card held in addition to a pair.

Limit: The maximum amount of a bet or raise.

Lowball: A variation of poker in which the low hand wins the pot. Also called low poker.

One pair: A hand consisting of a single pair along with three odd cards.

Open, open the betting: A player who makes the first bet on any particular round of betting; the player who must make the mandatory opening bet on the first betting round.

Open-ended straight: A four-straight that can be improved from either end, such as 6543.

Openers: In jacks or better, a hand that contains the minimum requirements for opening, after it has bet first.

Paint: See *Face card*.

Pass: See *Check*.

Pat hand: In draw poker, a hand that is sufficient without a card being drawn to it, such as a flush.

Pot: The amount of money or chips bet in total in any poker game.

Pot limit: A big-money game, in which a player may bet a sum equal to the total pot.

Raise: A bet made by a player that is greater than the previous bet made on the same betting round.

Rake: The amount of money withdrawn from each pot by the house in a casino game, or the percentage of the pot withdrawn.

Razz: The casino game of seven-card stud, lowball.

Reraise: Raising a previous raise on the same betting round.

Rough: A term to signify a high second- or third-card holding in lowball, such as a rough 8, which would be 87643.

Scoop, scoop a pot: Winning both the high and low of a high-low pot.

See a bet: See *Call*.

Showdown: The showing of the players' hands to determine who wins the pot after the last bet has been made.

Sixth Street: The next-to-last round of betting and play in a seven-card stud game.

Smooth: A lowball hand in which the second card is a low card, such as a smooth 8, which would be 8432A.

Stand pat: In draw poker, the refusal to draw a card to one's hand.

Straight: The holding of five consecutive cards of different suits, such as AKQJ10 or 98765.

Stud: A variation of poker in which some of the player's cards are exposed.

Sweeten the pot: See *Ante.*

Table stakes: Limiting the player to betting only money or chips he has on the table during a game of poker in action.

Third Street: The opening round of betting in seven-card stud.

Trips: The holding of three cards of one rank, such as 555. Also known as three of a kind.

Under the gun: The player who must act and bet first on any round of poker.

Wheel: See *Bicycle.*

Wild card: A card that can be designated as any card a player wishes, to improve his hand.